Lewis Helfand

ABRAHAM LINCOLN

FROM THE LOG CABIN TO THE WHITE HOUSE

KALYANI NAVYUG MEDIA PVT LTD

Abraham Lincoln

From the Log Cabin to the White House

Script
Lewis Helfand

Edits
Suparna Deb & Aditi Ray

Line Art
Manikandan

Color
Anil C. K.

Desktop Publishing
Bhavnath Chaudhary

www.campfire.co.in

Published by Kalyani Navyug Media Pvt. Ltd.
101 C, Shiv House, Hari Nagar Ashram, New Delhi 110014, India

ISBN: 978-93-80741-21-5

Printed in India

About the Author

Lewis Aaron Helfand has been interested in cartoons, animation, and comics from a young age, and by the age of twelve, had turned to writing in that medium as an amateur. His career, however, was a far cry from his passion. At the age of twenty-four, Lewis had been editing phonebooks for a year and a half and felt no closer to his lifelong goal of writing comic books. So, one day, he decided to quit his job.

Lewis then spent the next two months working day and night to write and draw his first independent comic book, *Wasted Minute*. It tells the story of a world without crime where superheroes are forced to work regular jobs. To cover the cost of self-publishing, he began working odd jobs in offices and restaurants, and started exhibiting his book at local comic book conventions. With the first issue received well, he was soon collaborating with other artists, and released four more issues over the next few years.

Outside the field of comics, Lewis works as a freelance writer and reporter for a number of US print and online publications. He has covered everything from sports and travel to politics and culture for magazines such as *Renaissance, American Health and Fitness,* and *Computer Bits*.

About the Artist

Hailing from Tamil Nadu, India, Manikandan was encouraged to pursue his artistic talents by his mother right from when he was a wee toddler. Even at a young age, he showed a natural aptitude for the often misunderstood world of comic book illustrations, and has since then honed his craft to better represent his ability. A Bachelor in Fine Arts from the College of Fine Arts, Chennai, Manikandan has worked with the biggest names in the comic book industry. His books for Campfire, such as *Sita: Daughter of the Earth* and *The Tempest*, are testimony to his versatility as a comic book artist.

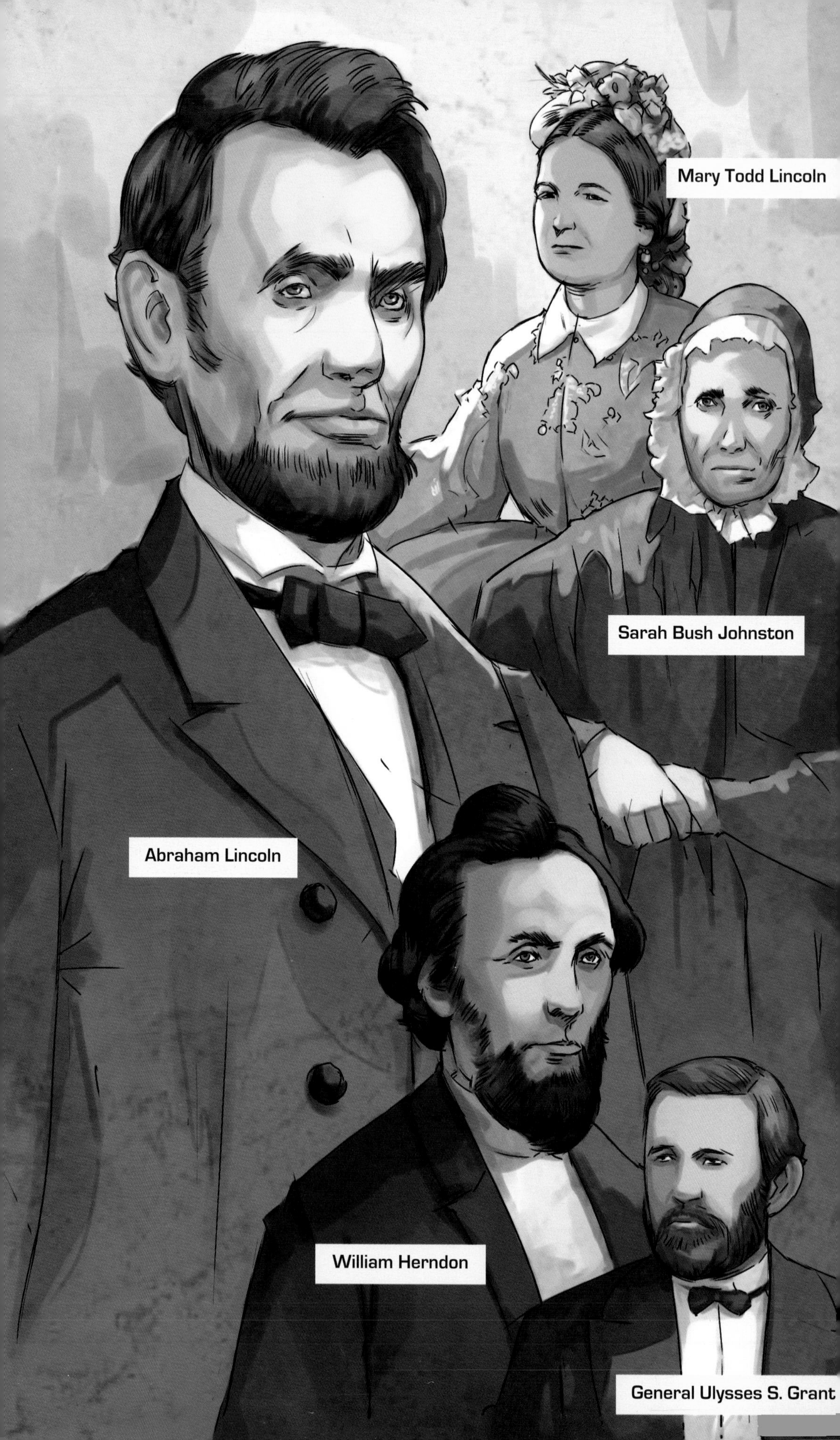
Mary Todd Lincoln
Sarah Bush Johnston
Abraham Lincoln
William Herndon
General Ulysses S. Grant

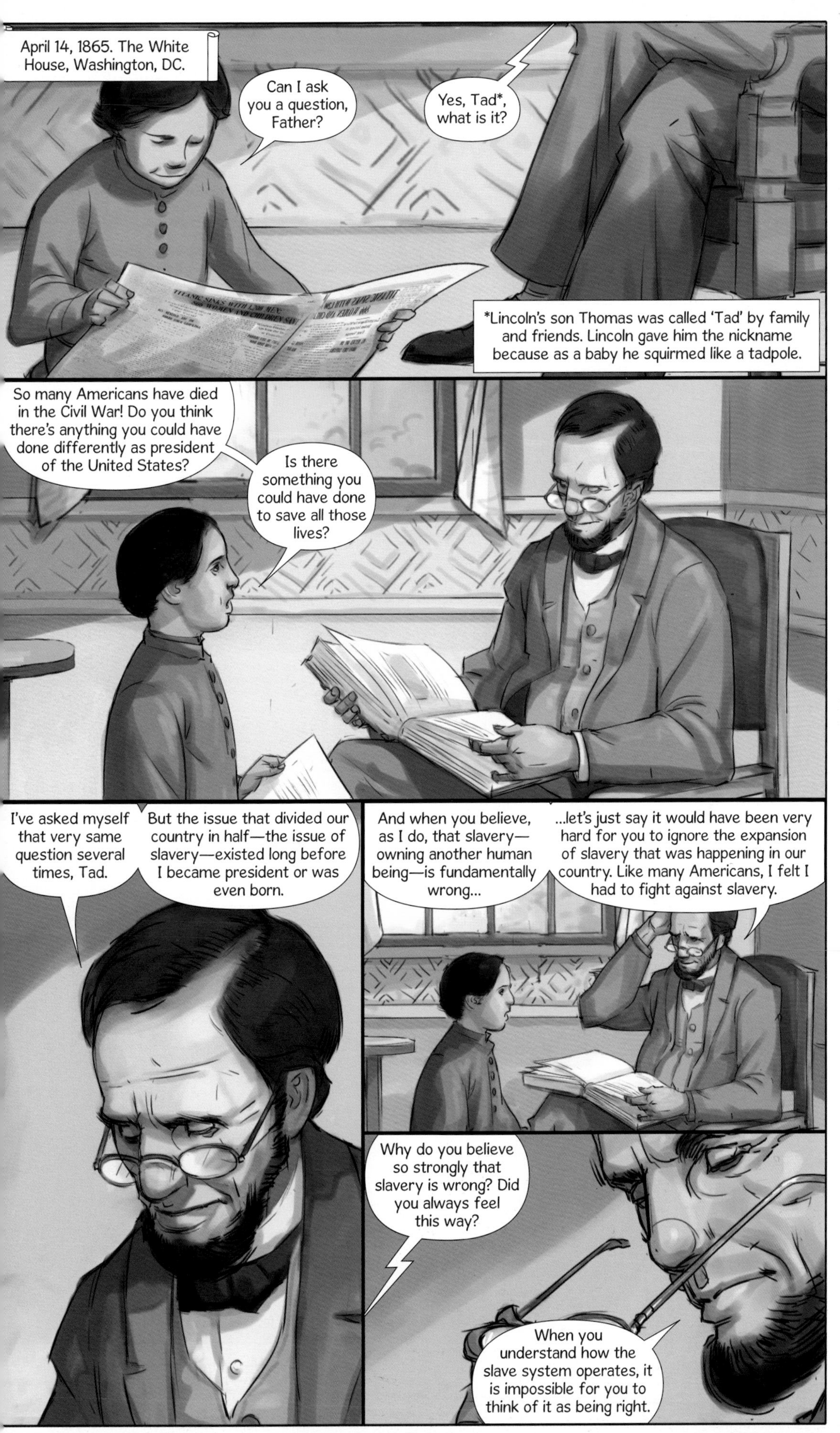
April 14, 1865. The White House, Washington, DC.
Can I ask you a question, Father?
Yes, Tad*, what is it?
*Lincoln's son Thomas was called 'Tad' by family and friends. Lincoln gave him the nickname because as a baby he squirmed like a tadpole.
So many Americans have died in the Civil War! Do you think there's anything you could have done differently as president of the United States?
Is there something you could have done to save all those lives?
I've asked myself that very same question several times, Tad.
But the issue that divided our country in half—the issue of slavery—existed long before I became president or was even born.
And when you believe, as I do, that slavery—owning another human being—is fundamentally wrong...
...let's just say it would have been very hard for you to ignore the expansion of slavery that was happening in our country. Like many Americans, I felt I had to fight against slavery.
Why do you believe so strongly that slavery is wrong? Did you always feel this way?
When you understand how the slave system operates, it is impossible for you to think of it as being right.

'Even before America was founded in 1776, much of our economy was based on farming, especially in the southern part of the country. And tending to the crops on these plantations was hard, grueling work.'
Men did not want to work on the fields or limit their profits by hiring many workers to tend the fields...'
'...so they turned to slavery, to the continent of Africa.'
'Men and women from Africa were forced from their homelands by the slave traders...'
On your feet!
'...and transported by ship to America to be sold to wealthy, white plantation owners to work on their fields.'
'Once enslaved, they had no freedom and no rights. They were paid nothing for their work, and were treated like animals or property.'

'Many people objected to the enslavement on moral or religious grounds. They wanted slavery outlawed.'
'But America was made up of several states, each free to make its own laws, which included those regarding slavery.'
'By 1809 there were twenty-two states in America. Those in the North did not allow slavery. But those in the South felt otherwise.'
'And whether all of the undeveloped land in the west of America would or wouldn't allow slavery was becoming perhaps the biggest question facing America then.'
'Every American had an opinion on whether slavery was right or wrong...'
'...including my parents.'
'But my parents, born to undistinguished families, weren't leaders looking to change the country. They just wanted to carve out their own quiet place and start a family.'
'And that is what they did. On February 12, 1809, in Hardin County in Kentucky, I was born in a small, one-room log cabin.'

1815. Knob Creek, Kentucky.
'Of course I wasn't aware of what was happening in our nation when I was a boy. My sister Sarah and my concerns then were with things like...'
What should we plant in our garden, Sarah?
Mother and Father said we could plant anything we want. Let's plant pumpkins that will grow bigger than our home!
And corn that will grow taller than our father!
'Unfortunately, a heavy rain soon flooded our little garden.'
Father!
Mother!
Can we plant new crops in our garden and watch them grow, Father?
Yes, we can, Abraham. But I'm not sure whether we will be here to see it grow.

'My father had purchased a farmland in Kentucky with the hope of raising crops and livestock to provide for his family.'
'But in Kentucky, the local government did not oversee land purchases. So at times, there were several people claiming ownership of one land, which led to bitter disputes.'
You say you purchased the land near the creek, Thomas, and that it has dried up. I say there never was a creek here. This land is mine!
'Over the years, my father lost a lot of land and money in disputes, like many living in Kentucky.'
'As my parents were poor and illiterate, they depended on land to survive.'
We should move to Indiana, Nancy.
In Indiana, no one can take our land from us, as the government regulates all land purchases.
I've also heard that Indiana is a free state, filled with people like us who believe slavery is unjust.
'About one-eighth of Americans were enslaved then—all of them black—and slavery was an issue weighing on the minds of **all** Americans.'
'So we moved to a new farm in Spencer County in Indiana in December 1816, and set up a small shelter to serve as our new home.'

'Indiana then was undeveloped—a frontier* state. Only woods and wild animals surrounded us.'
*The unexplored region beyond the towns and cities.
'We didn't even have a proper school to attend. As in Kentucky, education came only from ABC Schools*.'
'And that only when a teacher happened to pass through the frontier. In our entire childhood, my sister and I probably had only a year of schooling.'
A B C D E F G...
A B C D E F G...
ABCDEFG
*Schools teaching only the basics, like the alphabet.
'My mother would always encourage me to read, while my father wanted me to do other things.'
Come on, Abraham. You should be working!
'I did the work reluctantly, as I would much rather spend my time reading, which I loved.'

February 1817.
'I used to spend my days chopping wood to build fences for neighbors...'
THWACK
'...or collecting water or firewood, or plowing the fields for my parents...'
'...or sometimes hunting.'
BLAM!
I killed a turkey, Mother! It's dead because of me.
It will be alright, Abe. Death is a part of life.
Oh, no! What have I done?!
'I felt terrible, and never hunted again. As I was about to learn later, death was a very common part of life on the frontier.'

'In fact, death and illness were far too common, and my beloved mother grew gravely ill with little warning.'
Abe... Sarah... come close.
I want both of you to be good to your father.
And be kind to each other... always. And to the world.
'She had milk sickness, an illness caused by drinking the milk of a cow that had eaten toxic plants. The illness claimed my mother's life on October 5, 1818.'
'Living alone in the Indiana wilderness, miles from anyone, we had to make the coffin ourselves...'
'...and bury her ourselves without even a minister present.'
'Losing my mother at such a young age was terrible. The burden of the household fell on my sister, who was just eleven then.'

'We struggled through that winter and the following summer. After a period of mourning...'
I'm going to Kentucky, children. I will return as soon as I can.
'When my father returned a few weeks later, he was not alone.'
I'd like you to meet my two children, Abraham and Sarah.
Children, this is Sarah Bush Johnston... your new mother.
Oh, you poor things! I'll have to get the two of you cleaned up right away. But first...
...I want both of you to know that I am thrilled to be part of your family!
'My father and Sarah had got married on December 2, 1819, and together with her three children, she came to live with us.'

Thomas, you will have to do something about this cabin. There's no furniture.
Our children need a proper home, with a floor, windows, and a finished roof.
That's fine, Sarah. I have Abraham here to help me.
'Sarah was nice and treated us like her own children from the start.'
'I think she sensed that I wanted something more out of life.'
Do you like to read, Abe?
Have you read *The Arabian Nights*? I've also got *Aesop's Fables* and *Robinson Crusoe*. I think you'll like them.
'She encouraged me to read. She soon became the best friend I ever had. I owe all that I am to my angel stepmother.'

That boy is lazy, Sarah. He should be doing his chores. He's just wasting his time by reading. He's--
He's doing no such thing. He's educating himself, Thomas.
He wants to make something of himself. And you shouldn't stop him.
'Sarah **always** supported me. And I loved her for it.'
'With her encouragement, I began devouring every book I could lay my hands on. I read about some of the founders of our country like George Washington and Benjamin Franklin.'
'I read so much that I was able to overcome my lack of formal education. I even started reading poetry, Shakespeare, and the Bible.'
'I used to walk sixteen miles to the town of Rockport, where a local judge was kind enough to allow me to read whatever he had in his office.'
'Unlike the novels given to me by my stepmother, what I read there were mostly law books, which I equally enjoyed reading.'

'While I spent much of my time reading, I also managed to find time for other things, like competing with the boys in whatever game we could come up with.'
'Whether it was running a race, lifting heavy objects, wrestling, or simply splitting rails, I always took pride in being the best.'
'Best at **everything**.'
'Even storytelling. I had a pretty good memory, and since I read a lot, I had collected a wealth of jokes and stories that I was eager to share with my friends and siblings.'
'At times, I would even pretend to be a politician or preacher, and deliver sermons!'
'I doubt if I made a convincing politician or preacher back then. For it wasn't until a few years later, when I was a teenager, that I finally encountered a public speaker capable of captivating a crowd.'

'When I heard that John Brackenridge, a famous attorney, was coming to Boone, Indiana...'
'...I walked sixteen miles from home just to hear him speak in court.'
'He was there to defend a client charged with murder.'
Murder?! Why the mere idea of my client committing any crime, let alone one so heinous, it is absolutely absurd!
My client is an upstanding citizen, loved by his friends and neighbors, adored by his family. Your Honor, before this day is over...
...everyone in this room will be convinced that my client is an innocent man, guilty of no crime.
'I made it a point to meet Brackenridge after his defense.'
Mr. Brackenridge, it was an honor to hear you speak. Thank you.
'He was such a gifted speaker that I was inspired to become an attorney myself.'

'But how could I? I had practically no formal education; life on the frontier valued hard physical labor above everything else.'
'So I continued with the odd jobs, from plowing fields...'
'...to working in a general store for a local businessman called James Gentry.'
'It was all a series of mundane chores.'
January 20, 1828.
'We were all very happy when my dear sister, who had recently got married, became pregnant with her first child.'
'But she died while giving birth. And her child, a boy, was stillborn.'
No! Noooo!!!!
'It was devastating. But on the frontier, you had to push past the losses and keep working to survive. And that is what I had to do.'

April 1828.
'When Mr. Gentry wanted to deliver agricultural produce to New Orleans, he hired me to help his son Allen.'
'Edible produce was often sent there by river to be sold or traded since much of the Southern farms grew only sugar, tobacco, and cotton.'
'And there was always a high demand for food due to the numerous slaves who worked on the plantations. I took up the job thinking it would be easy.'
'And it was... until we docked near Baton Rouge in Louisiana for the night.'
Out of nowhere we were surrounded by seven black men intending to rob us.'
'Our best chance of escape lay in keeping the men off the boat.'
ARRRGGH!
ARRRGGH!
Luckily, we managed to do just that and got away relatively unharmed. Slavery had robbed the men of everything, and they must have thought it fair to employ any means to get what they could.'
'It was my first experience of the world far from the frontiers.'

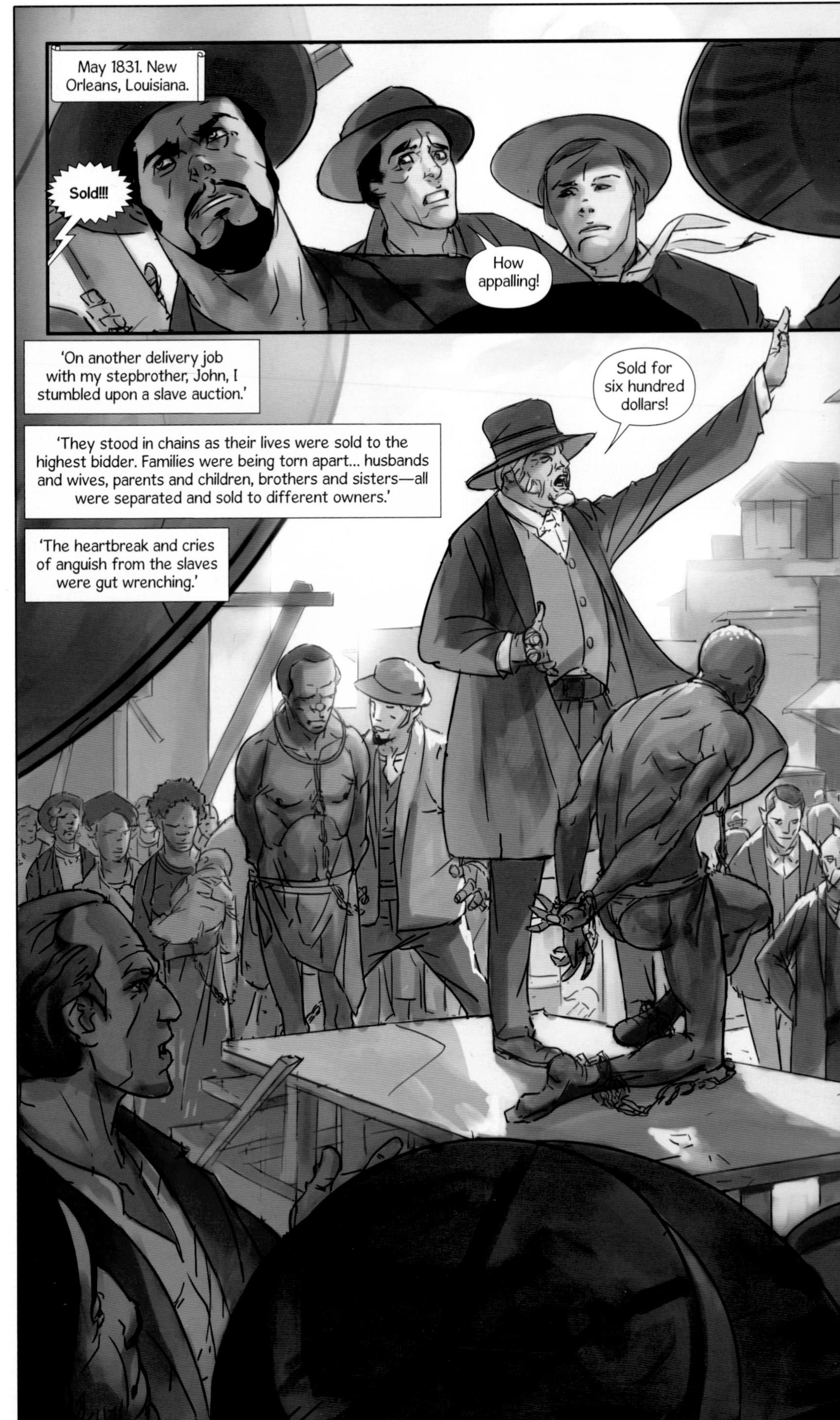
May 1831. New Orleans, Louisiana.
Sold!!!
How appalling!
'On another delivery job with my stepbrother, John, I stumbled upon a slave auction.'
Sold for six hundred dollars!
'They stood in chains as their lives were sold to the highest bidder. Families were being torn apart... husbands and wives, parents and children, brothers and sisters—all were separated and sold to different owners.'
'The heartbreak and cries of anguish from the slaves were gut wrenching.'

'I was horrified by the way the men and women were pinched and prodded like animals to determine how strong they were.'
This one will do.
'It made me wonder how anyone could look upon such a spectacle and not see that it was all wrong.'
'And that it continued to be permitted.'

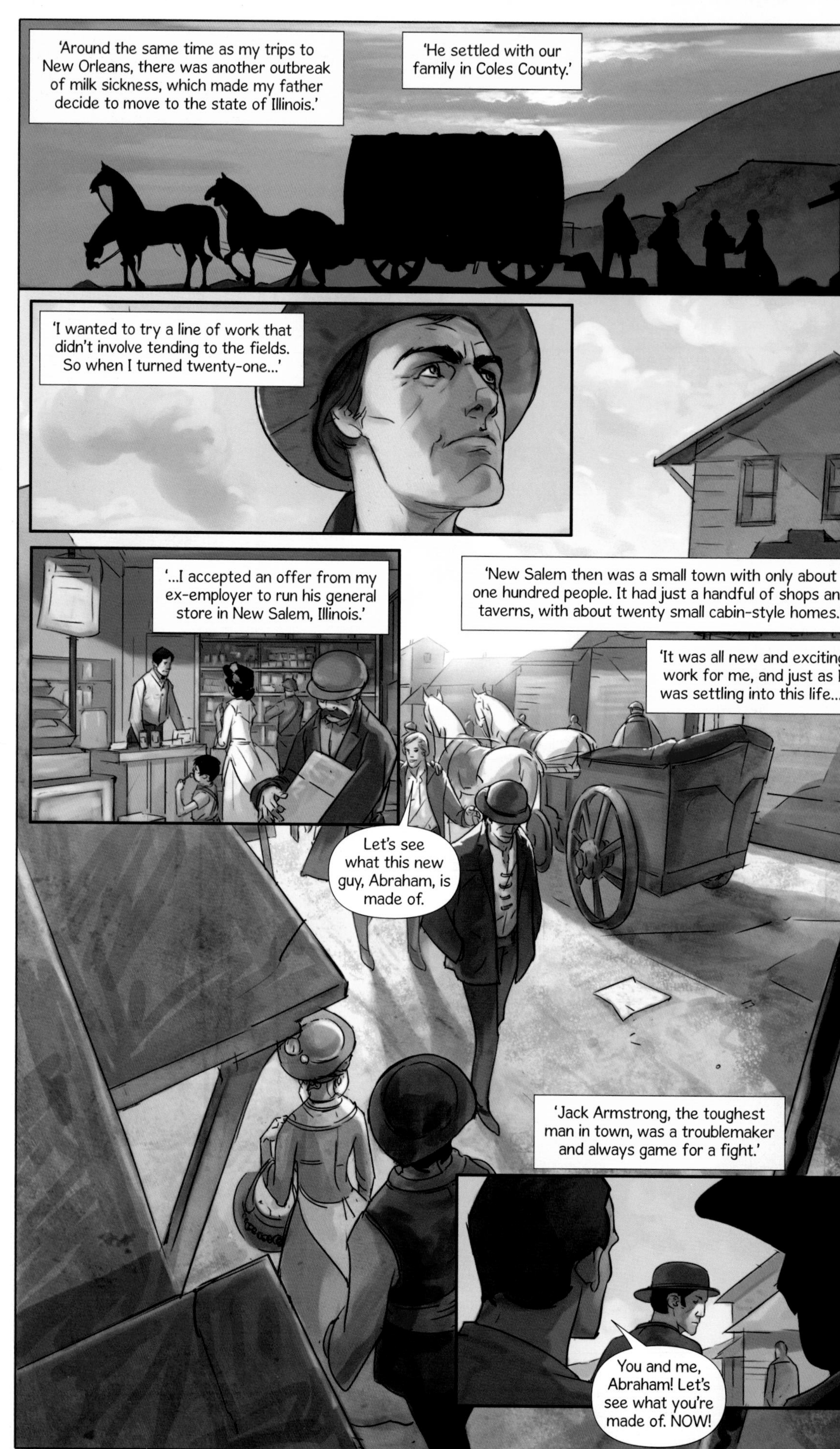
'Around the same time as my trips to New Orleans, there was another outbreak of milk sickness, which made my father decide to move to the state of Illinois.'
'He settled with our family in Coles County.'
'I wanted to try a line of work that didn't involve tending to the fields. So when I turned twenty-one...'
'...I accepted an offer from my ex-employer to run his general store in New Salem, Illinois.'
'New Salem then was a small town with only about one hundred people. It had just a handful of shops and taverns, with about twenty small cabin-style homes.'
'It was all new and exciting work for me, and just as I was settling into this life...'
Let's see what this new guy, Abraham, is made of.
'Jack Armstrong, the toughest man in town, was a troublemaker and always game for a fight.'
You and me, Abraham! Let's see what you're made of. NOW!

I have no grievance against you, Jack. And I, therefore, have no reason to fight you.
But if you like, I will not object to a wrestling match with some set rules.
'Jack agreed. His friends, who called themselves the Clary's Grove Boys, wagered money on Armstrong.'
Come on everybody, I'll take all bets!
This new guy, Abraham, is going down.
'Some of the townspeople thought I could win because of my size, and wagered on me.'
'One of the rules we had agreed upon was not to attack below the waist.'
'But that is exactly what Jack Armstrong did.'
Lincoln's down! Jack's the winner!
Everyone who bet on Lincoln owes us money. And you'd better pay up! Does anyone have a problem with that?
I was indeed taken down. And I have no problem with that, Jack. I congratulate you. But it was unfair.
So I think it would be dishonest to make those who bet on me pay when I was fouled. I didn't want to fight you, but I will fight you now in the name of fairness.

You've got guts, I'll give you that!
You're right, Abraham. I respect your nerve and there's no need for another fight. Good match.
Did you see how that Lincoln fellow didn't even care that he was fouled? He was willing to laugh about it.
And he spoke for us who had bet on him. He didn't want us to be cheated.
'I guess the people of New Salem were impressed by how I handled Jack.'
'For I always tried to do what I thought was right, whether it was during a wrestling match or working at the general store.'
Oh no!
I overcharged the customer by some cents. It's my mistake.
I should return his money right away. Why make him suffer for it.
'I walked a few miles to the customer's home that very night to return the money.'
'When I reached his house...'
You didn't have to come all the way out here to return my money. But I appreciate your being so honest, Abe!
'**Honest Abe**. From then on, that's what the townspeople called me.'

'I enjoyed my time in New Salem. I joined a debate team there, debating politics and the issues of the day. The best thing about it was that I was able to borrow books from all its members.'
It's a book of poetry by Robert Burns. I think you'll like it, Abe.
'The people of New Salem thought my reading was a sign of intelligence whereas my father thought it was just a waste of time and a sign of laziness.'
'And they respected the way I handled myself against Jack Armstrong and the way I treated the customers at the store.'
March 1832.
The election for state legislature is in August, and we need someone local to run and represent our interests.
So much of New Salem's economy depends on shipping produce along the Sangamon River. We need a representative to push for improving the canal, which is too shallow for our boats to navigate.
What about Abe? He's an honest guy and a good speaker. And he has worked on boats, delivering produce, and knows the problems we face.
Hey Abe!
Me? You want me to run for office? I am new here—it has hardly been a year.
'My lack of formal education made me doubt my abilities. But my friends thought otherwise.'
'So with their encouragement, I agreed to run for the state legislature as a member of the Whig political party. I announced my candidacy on March 9, 1832, but the election wasn't until August.'
Out of Business
'By then the store I worked in had closed down, and I was on the lookout for work.'

April 1832.
The Sauk Indians have crossed into Illinois in search of new land.
The governor is asking for volunteers to drive them back across the border.
'The Sauks, a local Indian tribe, who had been pushed out of their native lands in 1804, wanted to reclaim their old lands.'
'They were led by their chief whose name was Black Hawk, and so the war came to be known as the Black Hawk War.'
'I decided to volunteer for the war and joined a military unit, as did many from New Salem, including Jack Armstrong.'
Popular as ever, Abe. We would all like you t be our captain.
I'm honored. How would you like to be my first sergeant?
Count me in. I'm ready to see some combat, Abe!
I think we will see a lot of that, Jack.
'I made a number of new friends in my unit like John Todd Stuart, a lawyer from Springfield, Illinois. But as for combat...'
It's been three months, and we haven't seen a single Indian, let alone fight any battle.
I think I should head back to New Salem now John. It's time fo the elections.

August 6, 1832.
New Salem, Illinois.
'Despite the support of my friends and New Salem residents, I did not do well in my first election.'
Vote for Abraham Lincol
'I came in eighth out of thirteen candidates. However, I did not let the loss weigh me down. There were too many good things happening in my life then.'
A few months later. 1833.
'Perhaps the best thing was Anne Rutledge. Her family ran a local tavern and boarding house where I sometimes rented a room.'
Are you free tomorrow night, Anne?
Tomorrow night?! Why Abe, if you want to see me this frequently, I'm going to get the impression that you like me.
You didn't answer my question.
Yes, Abe. I'm free to see you tomorrow night.

'With the next election not until August 1834, I tried my hand at all kinds of work, from helping a local blacksmith...'
'...to opening my own general store with a partner. However, the store didn't fare well, and soon went out of business.'
'I then became New Salem's postmaster. Our town received very little mail, and many a times I would keep the letters under my hat and deliver them as I walked through town.'
'What I enjoyed most about the job was that I got the chance to read the newspapers that came from all over the country, before I delivered them.'
'With mail coming in only twice a week, the job offered me plenty of spare time to read and talk about politics—an ideal situation since standing for elections was still my focus.'
More than one representative is neede for the legislature, so you'll still be able to serve even if you come in second or third in the election, Abe.
I know. The chance to serve our community is what I want.

'And on August 4, 1834, I was elected General Assemblyman. The capitol building of Illinois was in Vandalia at the time, a two-day journey from New Salem.'
'I had to travel up and down from Vandalia to New Salem for my new role.'
'I used to share a room in Vandalia with my friend John Todd Stuart, who had been elected to the legislature too.'
You know, when I was younger, I wanted to become a lawyer like you. But it just remained a dream.
Why don't you become one now?
But I have had very little schooling, John.
You shouldn't let that discourage you, Abe. If you **really** want to be a lawyer, that's the path you should follow.
I'd be happy to help you. I've got several legal books which I could loan you. You really should try, Abe.

February 1835. New Salem, Illinois.
'And so with John's encouragement, I set my sights on becoming a lawyer and began studying as much as I could after the legislative session ended.'
Blackstone's Commentaries
'I also spent a lot of time with Anne. Many in New Salem assumed we would marry after I received my law degree.'
'But unfortunately Anne had typhoid...'
'...and never recovered from it. She died on August 25, 1835.'
'Losing Anne almost destroyed me. For months, I couldn't shake off the sadness and depression.'

A year later, I was re-elected to the state legislature, and on September 9, 1836, I received my license to practice law. But it was still a struggle to keep my spirits up.'
'Luckily for me, everyone around me tried to help me through my depression. Like Elizabeth Abell, Anne's neighbor.'
I know you miss her, Abe. We all do. Be strong.
I miss Anne so much, Elizabeth. I can't even stand the idea of the rain beating down upon her grave.
'Elizabeth invited me to her place, and that is how I met her sister, Mary Owens.'
'Mary was from my home state of Kentucky, and had come to New Salem that year to visit her sister.'
I will get you some coffee, Abe.
'We would often see each other, and I began to enjoy her company. But I still could not shake off my sorrow.'
'Luckily for me, I still had good friends who were determined to see me pull through.'
What you need is a fresh start, Abe. Why don't you move to Springfield and join me...
...as a partner in my law firm. Think about it.
'I gave John's offer some thought and decided to move.'

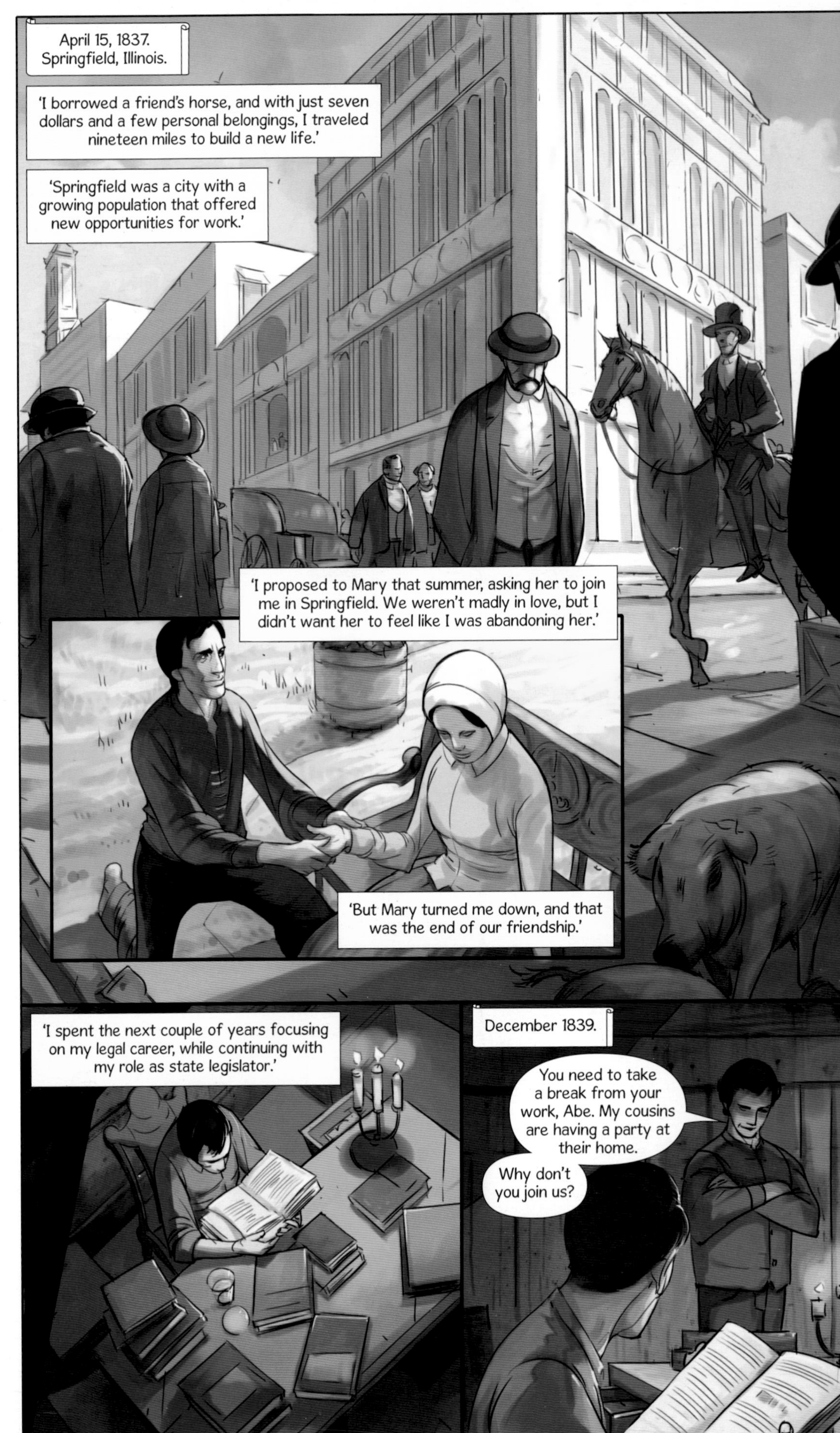
April 15, 1837.
Springfield, Illinois.
'I borrowed a friend's horse, and with just seven dollars and a few personal belongings, I traveled nineteen miles to build a new life.'
'Springfield was a city with a growing population that offered new opportunities for work.'
'I proposed to Mary that summer, asking her to join me in Springfield. We weren't madly in love, but I didn't want her to feel like I was abandoning her.'
'But Mary turned me down, and that was the end of our friendship.'
'I spent the next couple of years focusing on my legal career, while continuing with my role as state legislator.'
December 1839.
You need to take a break from your work, Abe. My cousins are having a party at their home.
Why don't you join us?

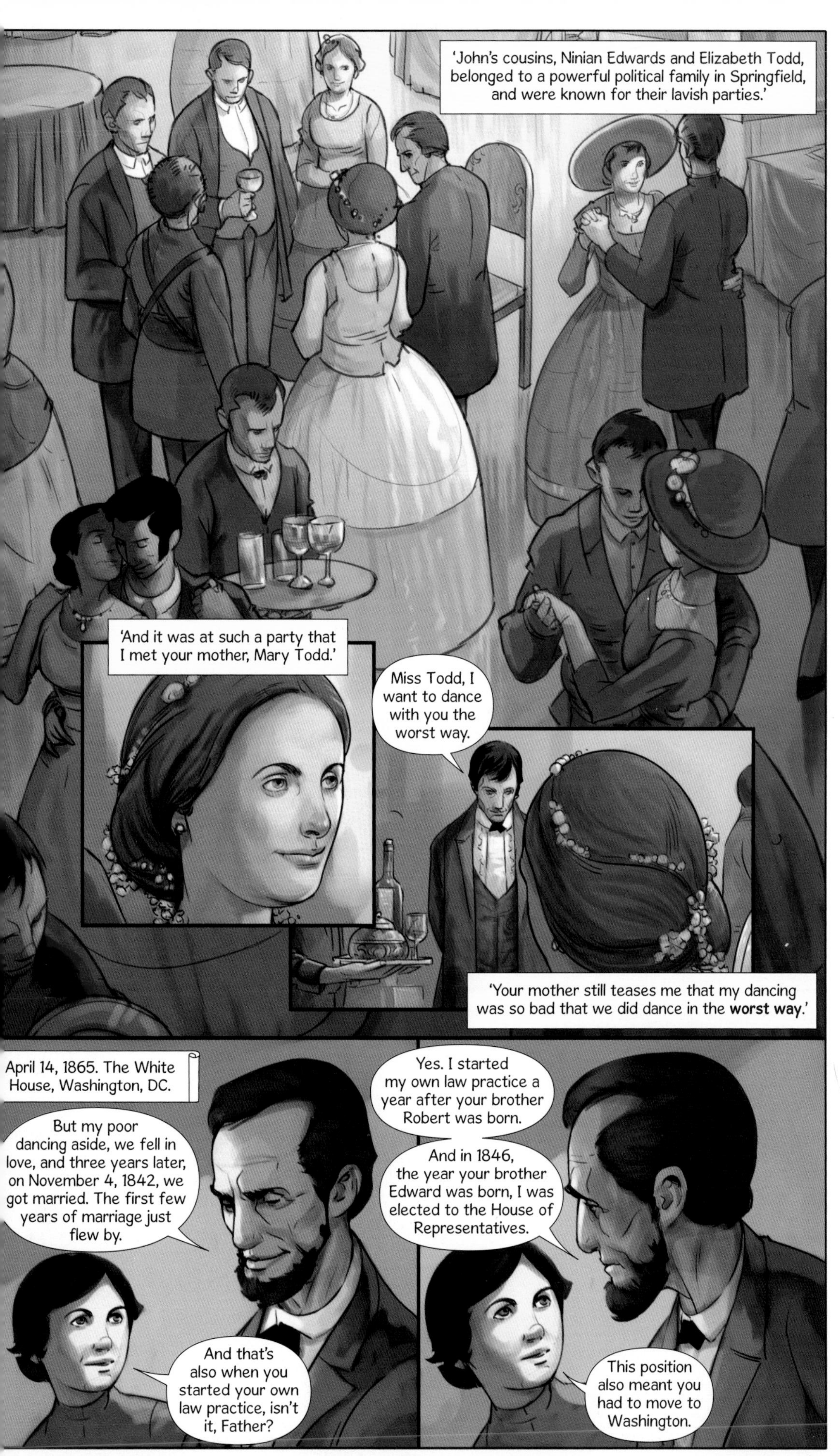
'John's cousins, Ninian Edwards and Elizabeth Todd, belonged to a powerful political family in Springfield, and were known for their lavish parties.'
'And it was at such a party that I met your mother, Mary Todd.'
Miss Todd, I want to dance with you the worst way.
'Your mother still teases me that my dancing was so bad that we did dance in the **worst way**.'
April 14, 1865. The White House, Washington, DC.
But my poor dancing aside, we fell in love, and three years later, on November 4, 1842, we got married. The first few years of marriage just flew by.
And that's also when you started your own law practice, isn't it, Father?
Yes. I started my own law practice a year after your brother Robert was born.
And in 1846, the year your brother Edward was born, I was elected to the House of Representatives.
This position also meant you had to move to Washington.

1847. Washington, DC.
Robert, this is the US Capitol building. This is where I'm going to work from now on.
This is where men from all over the country gather to make laws and decide what is just.
'I still remembered the day I had witnessed a slave auction. I was horrified to learn that Washington, DC itself was home to 2,000 slaves, and the largest slave trading house in the country.'
'During my two-year tenure in the Congress, I was bent upon introducing legislation to ban slavery in Washington, DC.'
'I began meeting other politicians, senators, and the mayor of Washington, DC to gain their support.'
The country looks to Washington for leadership.
We should be embarrassed that we permit slavery to exist in this city.
Do you not understand that no man has the right to own another?
'Unfortunately many thought otherwise, and would not support my proposal. And without the support of other lawmakers, I knew my legislation would not be passed.'

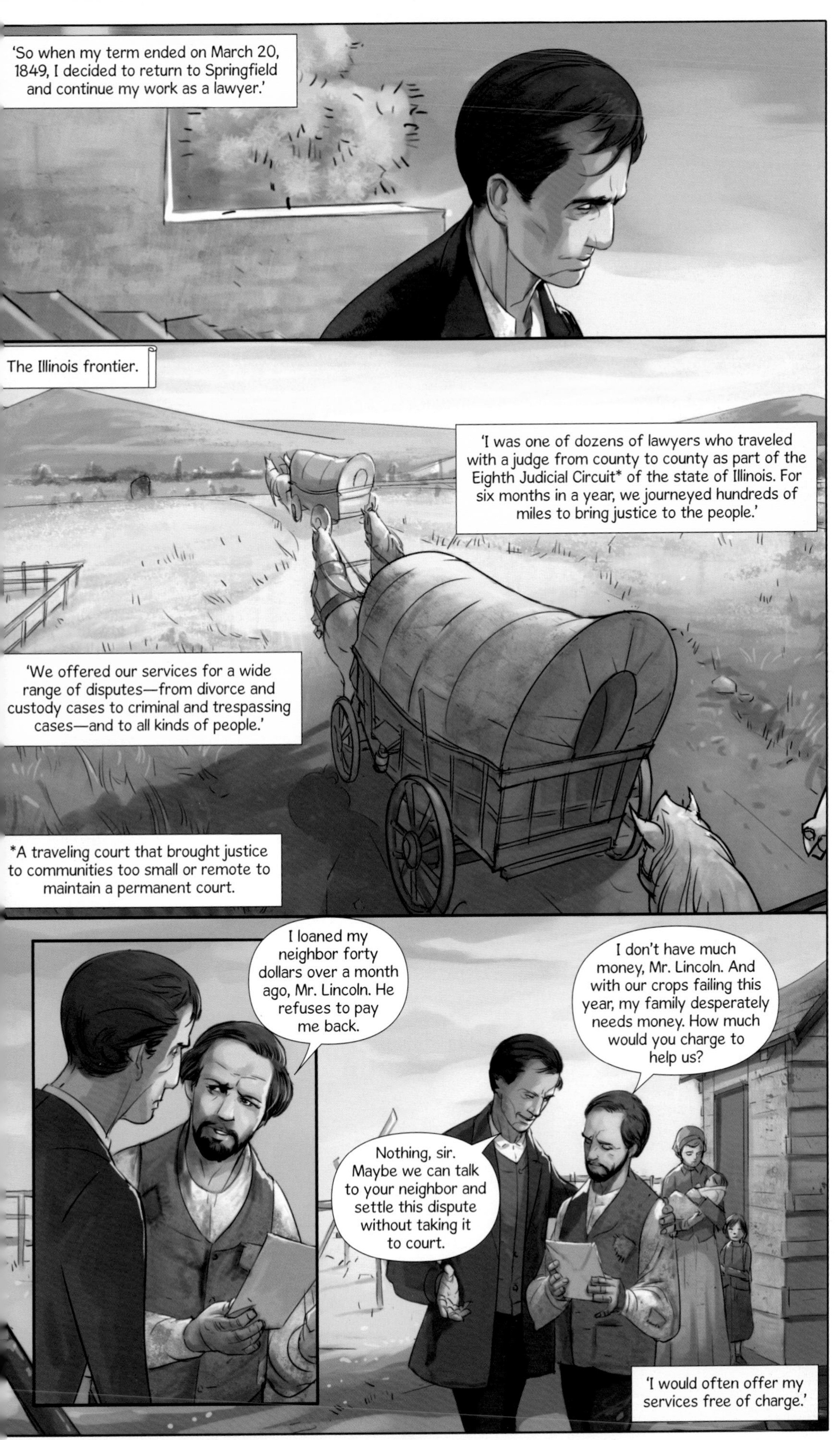
'So when my term ended on March 20, 1849, I decided to return to Springfield and continue my work as a lawyer.'
The Illinois frontier.
'I was one of dozens of lawyers who traveled with a judge from county to county as part of the Eighth Judicial Circuit* of the state of Illinois. For six months in a year, we journeyed hundreds of miles to bring justice to the people.'
'We offered our services for a wide range of disputes—from divorce and custody cases to criminal and trespassing cases—and to all kinds of people.'
*A traveling court that brought justice to communities too small or remote to maintain a permanent court.
I loaned my neighbor forty dollars over a month ago, Mr. Lincoln. He refuses to pay me back.
I don't have much money, Mr. Lincoln. And with our crops failing this year, my family desperately needs money. How much would you charge to help us?
Nothing, sir. Maybe we can talk to your neighbor and settle this dispute without taking it to court.
'I would often offer my services free of charge.'

'On the road for months at a time with just the lawyers and judges for company, we all became very close and joked around like brothers.'
Look, Ward Hill Lamon is presenting his case with a large tear in his pants.
Yes, he ripped his pants while wrestling with another lawyer outside the courthouse. He didn't have time to change his clothing.
Wouldn't it be fun if we collected some money for him to buy new pants? Let us all pledge some money for the cause.
HA HA HA HA
'We had a few good times together.'
I pledge two dollars to help Ward purchase new pants—Leonard Swett
I pledge three dollars for Ward's pants—Henry Clay Whitney
I can contribute nothing to the end in view—
A. Lincoln
'But nothing could match up to the times when I was able to return home to my family.'
I missed all of you so much, Eddie.

February 1, 1850.
Springfield, Illinois.
'As wonderful as it was to be back home, nothing could ease the devastation when your brother Edward became ill with consumption*.'
'He died at the age of three.'
Not my Eddie! Not my boy! I can't bear losing him!
*Pulmonary tuberculosis.
Angel Boy, fare thee well,
Farewell Sweet Eddie.
We bid thee adieu!
Affection's wail cannot reach thee now
Deep though it be, and true.
Bright is the home to him now given
For of such is the Kingdom of Heaven.

'But our loss gave way to better times when your brother William Wallace was born that year, and three years later, you were born.'
'I remember when you both were still young and used to visit my office. The two of you would tear through my office and go through everything.'
'The mess you caused used to frustrate both your mother and my legal partner, William Herndon.'
I hope you are going to punish them for this, Abe?
No. It is my pleasure that my children are free— happy and unrestrained by parental tyranny.

January 1854.
This is an **outrage**!
Have you read this, Mary? Our government had passed some laws years ago which kept some of the western territories free of slavery.
Now Senator Stephen A. Douglas of Illinois is proposing what he calls the Kansas-Nebraska Act which would change those laws and allow each territory to decide whether they want to permit slavery.
This means that slavery could spread to **every** western territory. **Slavery is wrong**, Mary. This law is wrong. I have to oppose it. I have to stop it from being implemented.
October 16, 1854. Peoria, Illinois.
'Despite my protests, the law was passed in May that year. But I continued speaking out publicly against the expansion of slavery across Illinois.'
Slavery is founded on the selfishness of man's nature—opposition to it on his love of justice.
No man is good enough to govern another man, without that other's consent.
I don't know much about this Lincoln guy, but I support his views on slavery completely.
Yeah, so do I.

1858. Beardstown, Illinois.
'My crusade against slavery continued for four more years while I worked as a lawyer.'
My client, William Duff Armstrong, has been accused of committing murder on the night of August 29, 1857.
'Duff was the son of my old friend Jack Armstrong. Jack had passed away before the trial, and I took up the case for free as a favor to the family.'
Mr. Charles Allen here is the chief witness against my client. Mr. Allen, are you positive you saw **everything** that happened on the night in question?
Yes, I witnessed William Duff Armstrong commit murder. I was probably fifty yards away.
The full moon that night lit up the land bright enough for me to see as if it was day.
Unlucky for my client, for otherwise, at that distance it would have been impossible to see anything clearly at night.
And yet look at this. I hold in my hands an 1857 almanac. And according to this book...
The Old Farmer's Almanac 1857
...there was only a quarter moon that night, too low on the horizon for Mr. Allen to see anything clearly.
Mr Armstrong is found not guilty!!!
'Even though my reputation as a lawyer was growing, it took a backseat to my renewed political ambitions.'

June 16, 1858.
Springfield, Illinois.
'Democratic senator Stephen A. Douglas believed there was nothing wrong with expanding the practice of slavery. So when he came up for re-election for a third term, I decided to run against him.'
'I was running for the brand new Republican Party, made up of some former Whigs and others opposed to slavery.'
A house divided against itself cannot stand. I believe this government cannot endure, permanently half slave and half free.
I do not expect the Union to be dissolved—I do not expect the house to fall—but I do expect it will cease to be divided.
It will become all one thing, or all the other.
'By July, both Senator Douglas and I had begun traveling across the state, trying to reach out to as many people as possible.'
'I challenged Senator Douglas that instead of the two of us speaking to different crowds at different times in different cities...'
'...we should face each other in a series of debates and have the chance to respond to each other directly.'

'So between August 21 and October 15, 1858, we managed to meet seven times in seven different towns in Illinois. Since we were addressing the biggest issue of the day...'
'...we not only attracted the local crowds, but also the attention of the entire country.'
'Because of the differences in our height and build, the debates were labeled The Little Giant vs Tall Abe or Honest Abe.'
'Each debate lasted three hours as we took turns delivering speeches, and then responded to the points that had been made.'
'Even rain could not keep the crowds away.'

Mr. Lincoln tells you, in his speech at Springfield, that 'a house divided against itself cannot stand'.
Why cannot this government endure, divided into free and slave states, as our fathers made it? Slavery is...
Slavery is wrong. It's inhumane and unjust. Whenever I hear anyone arguing for slavery, I feel a strong impulse to see it tried on him personally.
The right of each state to decide the slavery question for themselves is a sovereign right.
A sovereign right? If God meant for one class of citizens to do all the work and another class of citizens to get all the benefits, then he would have made workers with all hands and no mouth.
Mr. Lincoln admits that under the Constitution, on all domestic questions except slavery, we ought not to interfere with the people of the states. But I ask, what right have we to interfere with slavery any more than we have to interfere with any other question?
If slavery is not wrong, nothing is wrong.

January 1859.
Stephen Douglas defeats Lincoln to win re-election! Read all about it!
'Even though I lost the Senate race that time, my political reputation actually grew after my defeat. My speeches gave me a reputation nationwide as someone who was articulate and intelligent—a new face on the political scene.'
'Republicans from all over the country began wondering if I might make a good choice to run for president. My lack of experience in Washington worked as a plus, as I was an unknown among our political opponents.'
'So Republican leaders began inviting me to speak to crowds in Wisconsin, Ohio, Indiana, and...'
February 27, 1860. Cooper Union in Manhattan, New York.
The Democrats say we should cease to call slavery wrong, and join them in calling it right. Thinking it right, as they do, they are not to blame for desiring its full recognition as being right; but thinking it wrong, as we do, can we yield to them?
No! We will not yield!
We will not yield!
CLAP!
CLAP!
Let us have faith that right makes might, and in that faith, let us, to the end, dare to do our duty as we understand it.

'The convention to nominate the Republican presidential candidate was held in Chicago on May 18, 1860. While I remained in Springfield tending to my work...'
'...my friends William Herndon, Judge David Davis from the judicial circuit, and others traveled to Chicago to gain support for me.'
Seward, I say! William Seward for president!
New York senator William H. Seward, is in the lead by more than seventy votes, David.
I know, William. But Seward hasn't won the nomination yet. And Abe is in second place, ehind Seward and ahead of Ohio governor, Salmon P. Chase.
The delegations will have to vote again until one candidate receives enough votes.
Lincoln for president!
'The votes were cast a second time, and then a third, as men on the roof of the convention hall shouted updates to the crowd waiting outside for the results.'
'After the third round of voting, Lincoln has 231.5* of the 233 votes needed. But they might not have to vote again because...
*In many presidential nominating conventions, each delegate was given half a vote.
...it looks like a few people might change their votes.'
Lincoln is nominated!
Hurrah for Lincoln!
'And so I became the Republican candidate for the presidential elections.'

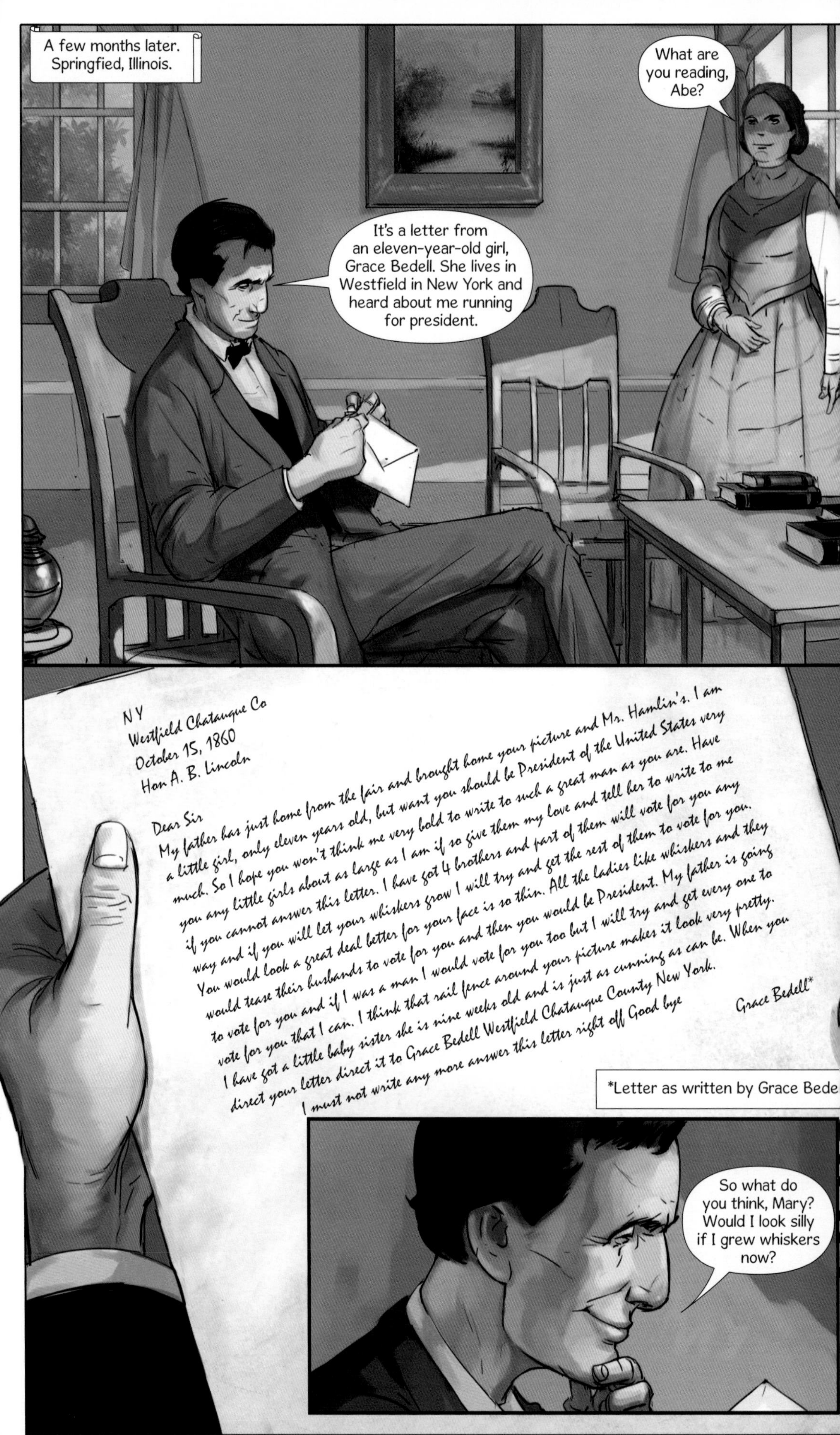
A few months later.
Springfied, Illinois.
What are you reading, Abe?
It's a letter from an eleven-year-old girl, Grace Bedell. She lives in Westfield in New York and heard about me running for president.
N Y
Westfield Chatauque Co
October 15, 1860
Hon A. B. Lincoln
Dear Sir
My father has just home from the fair and brought home your picture and Mr. Hamlin's. I am
a little girl, only eleven years old, but want you should be President of the United States very
much. So I hope you won't think me very bold to write to such a great man as you are. Have
you any little girls about as large as I am if so give them my love and tell her to write to me
if you cannot answer this letter. I have got 4 brothers and part of them will vote for you any
way and if you will let your whiskers grow I will try and get the rest of them to vote for you.
You would look a great deal better for your face is so thin. All the ladies like whiskers and they
would tease their husbands to vote for you and then you would be President. My father is going
to vote for you and if I was a man I would vote for you too but I will try and get every one to
vote for you that I can. I think that rail fence around your picture makes it look very pretty.
I have got a little baby sister she is nine weeks old and is just as cunning as can be. When you
direct your letter direct it to Grace Bedell Westfield Chatauque County New York.
I must not write any more answer this letter right off Good bye
Grace Bedell*
*Letter as written by Grace Bede
So what do you think, Mary? Would I look silly if I grew whiskers now?

'Of course I took little Grace's advice. I needed all the votes I could get.'
Did you see the news, Abe? It's now official. You'll be running against your old rival.
'The Democratic party had split in half, with Southern Democrats backing the pro-slavery John C. Breckinridge and the Northern Democrats supporting Stephen Douglas.'
'Douglas was still advocating the right of each new territory to decide the slavery issue for itself—a policy that proved more popular in the South than mine.'
Lincoln is calling for no slavery in the western territories. He won't get support with a platform like that!
'From North Carolina...'
'...to South Carolina...'
Ending slavery in the western territories won't be enough for him. If he's elected, he'll try to stop slavery in the South too. Take my word for that.
'...to Georgia and beyond...'
We need to ensure Lincoln isn't elected! We won't allow his name on the ballot.
My family, living in seven different states of the South, tells me Lincoln has zero support across the South.
'Ten Southern states actually struck my name off their ballots. And more than half of all Americans voting cast their votes for one of my opponents.'

November 6, 1860.
Springfield, Illinois.
'However, in the Northern states and even in some of the western territories, there were countless others who did support me, who believed as I did that slavery was wrong, that our country could not succeed with the population divided into free men and slaves.'
'My backing in the North was so strong that I won the election, though only 80 percent of the men* voted.'
The next president of our great nation. Well deserved, Abe. We're all thrilled for you. This is a time to celebrate!
VOTE FOR LINCOLN
VOTE FOR LINCOLN
'It was a time to celebrate for my friends and family. But for me it was a time for questions and doubts.'
What will happen when I finally take office? Will the Southern states, which have fought so hard to keep me from becoming president, now support me? Will they support my policies?'
Or because of my stand against slavery, they will oppose me every step of the way?
*Women did not have voting rights in the US at that time.

December 20, 1860. South Carolina.
'The answer to my questions came before I even took office, when 169 members of South Carolina's legislature met to discuss my upcoming inauguration.'
Lincoln wants to end slavery in the western territories. But it will not end there, I promise you that. He wants to end slavery everywhere!
Our economy depends on slave labor. Why, there must be 4 million slaves in the entire South! If Lincoln ends slavery... what will become of us?
Lincoln as president means an end to our way of life, an end to our prospering economy.
Then perhaps Lincoln should **not** be our president. We could secede from the Union.
And form our own government with our own laws. South Carolina would no longer be part of the United States, no longer be subject to Lincoln's policies.
All those in agreement?
AYE!
AYE!
AYE!
'Unfortunately it wasn't just South Carolina residents who felt they could not endure me as president.'

'All through the Southern states, one of the main sources of income were the cotton plantations.'
'It was a lucrative crop, which brought a lot of business from overseas—textile mills in England and France, for example.
'But harvesting cotton was labor intensive. And outlawing slavery, forcing plantation owners to cut into their profits to pay thousands of workers required to tend to their fields...'
'...was unacceptable to many in the South. So fearing I had plans to do exactly that, they decidec to form their own nation and government.'
'They decided they didn't want to improve the horrid living and working conditions of their slave labor.'
'Three weeks later, South Carolina secedec from the Union, and Mississippi, Florida, anc Alabama also followed soon after.'
'Over the next few weeks, the states of Georgi Louisiana, and Texas did the same, leaving just twenty-seven of thirty-four states in the Unior

'I wasn't even in office yet, and I was watching the nation I was supposed to lead crumble around me. I knew that I had to find a solution.'
'So I wrote to one of the most intelligent and capable men I could think of—New York senator William H. Seward.'
Who is the letter from, Father?
It's from Abraham Lincoln, Frederick. He is asking for my help.
Your help?! Didn't he run against you in the Republican primary? Didn't he defeat you in the presidential nomination?
Quite right. And now he is asking me to be part of his cabinet and become his secretary of state.
He is asking me to set aside our differences and join him in Washington.

'Seward accepted my request, and I turned my attention towards filling the rest of my cabinet. I wanted the best people on board.'
John Bunn, my old friend. How are you today?
I'm well, Abe. But was that Ohio governor, Salmon P. Chase, I just saw coming out of your office?
Why yes, it was. I invited him here to ask him to be secretary of the treasury in my cabinet.
You what? Abe, you need to rethink that. Chase is an ambitious man.
He probably resents that he lost the Republican presidential nomination to you. He probably thinks he's better and brighter than you are.
Really? Do you know any more men like that?
I do not. Why?
Because I'd like them in my cabinet as well.
I need the **best**, John. I don't care if they were my rivals or still are. I don't care if they are from different parties. We have to work together to save our country from falling apart.

February 4, 1861. Montgomery, Alabama.
'While I was busy forming my new government, the Southern states were doing the same.'
'Delegates from all seven seceding states joined together to form the Confederate States of America.'
'They even elected their own president, Jefferson Davis of Mississippi.'
'And as the South seceded, the Southerners began seizing every federal fort within their states, and its stock of arsenal.'
'It was as if they were preparing for an impending war.'
'With my inauguration just a month away, I decided to visit my beloved stepmother...'
What if someone doesn't like your policies and tries to hurt you, Abe?
I'll be fine. There's nothing to worry about.
'...and my friend and legal partner.'
Lincoln & Herndon
Good luck in Washington, Abe.
'On my way to Washington, I even made a stop at Westfield in New York to meet Miss Grace Bedell.'
Gracie, look at my whiskers. Would all the ladies like me now?
The whiskers suit you, Mr. Lincoln.
'I reached Philadelphia in Pennsylvania and met with a well-respected private detective, Allan Pinkerton.'
There is a plot to kill you, sir.

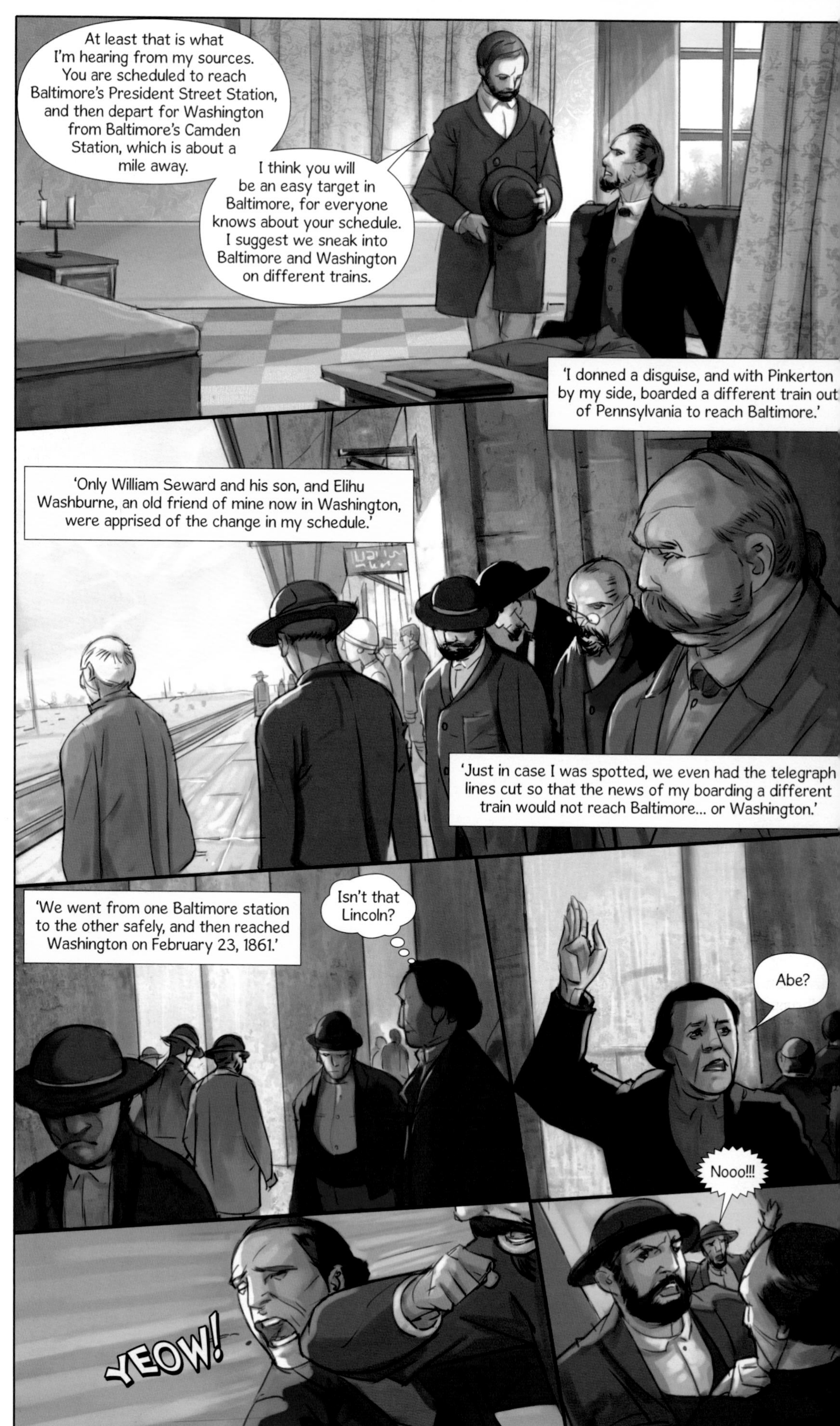
At least that is what I'm hearing from my sources. You are scheduled to reach Baltimore's President Street Station, and then depart for Washington from Baltimore's Camden Station, which is about a mile away.
I think you will be an easy target in Baltimore, for everyone knows about your schedule. I suggest we sneak into Baltimore and Washington on different trains.
'I donned a disguise, and with Pinkerton by my side, boarded a different train out of Pennsylvania to reach Baltimore.'
'Only William Seward and his son, and Elihu Washburne, an old friend of mine now in Washington, were apprised of the change in my schedule.'
'Just in case I was spotted, we even had the telegraph lines cut so that the news of my boarding a different train would not reach Baltimore... or Washington.'
'We went from one Baltimore station to the other safely, and then reached Washington on February 23, 1861.'
Isn't that Lincoln?
Abe?
Nooo!!!
YEOW!

Don't hurt him! That's my friend, Elihu Washburne.
I just wanted to make sure you got into Washington safely, Abe.
'Luckily, I reached Washington without any incident, and over the next couple of weeks, prepared for my inauguration.'
March 4, 1861. Washington, DC. Inauguration Day.
'30,000 people showed up to see me sworn in as president and to hear my first words to our troubled nation.'
'I suppose with America split in half, citizens were fearful that the divide might grow bigger, and they were waiting for me to provide a bit of hope and direction.'
Fellow citizens of the United States...
Apprehension seems to exist among the people of the Southern states that by the accession of a Republican administration, their property, peace, and personal security will be endangered.
There has never been any reasonable cause for such apprehension.

In your hands, my dissatisfied fellow countrymen, and not in mine, is the momentous issue of civil war. The government will not assail you.
You can have no conflict, without being yourselves the aggressors. You have no oath registered in heaven to destroy the government, while I shall have the most solemn one to preserve, protect, and defend it.
We are not enemies, but friends. We must not be enemies.
Though passion may have strained, it must not break our bonds of affection.
The mystic chords of memory, stretching from every battlefield and patriot grave to every living heart and hearthstone all over this broad land...
...will yet swell the chorus of the Union, when again touched, as surely they will be by the better angels of our nature.
What a tremendous speech!
I'm confident Lincoln can guid our fractured nation.

'The inauguration went off well, but just one month after taking office, on April 6, 1861, my worst fears were realized.'
I bring news about Fort Sumter, Mr. President. It is in dire need of supplies and reinforcements.
'Fort Sumter, a Union fort located in the harbor of Charleston in South Carolina, was one of only two Union forts in the South that had not yet been seized by the secessionists.'
'And being isolated in the hostile South, the soldiers inside Fort Sumter had only enough food to last them a few weeks.'
Send this letter to the governor of South Carolina. I am sending provisions to the soldiers at Fort Sumter—only provisions, not weapons and reinforcement.
'But the Confederate leaders would not allow fresh supplies to reach Fort Sumter, an 'enemy' fort off their own coast.'
'On April 12, before the supply ships even reached the fort, Confederate ships opened fire on the fort.'
'Within two days, the soldiers surrendered.'
'I had not fired the first shot, but I had also promised to preserve, protect, and defend my nation.'
April 15, 1861.
Call up more troops. We will put an end to this Southern rebellion.

'It was the beginning of the Civil War.'
I want our ships to set up a blockade of Southern ports to prevent the Confederate ships from leaving or supply ships from entering.
'In response to my actions, four more Southern states seceded over the next month—Virginia, Arkansas, Tennessee, and North Carolina. Fort Sumter was just the start of the rebellion.'
'Farmers and butchers and blacksmiths began arming themselves, preparing to become soldiers and fight the war.'
'Peaceful men became warriors, not only in the South, but in the North as well, with neither side willing to back down.'
BLAM!!

'In the North, white abolitionists and free blacks, many of whom were former slaves, wanted me to end slavery in all America, and not just prevent its expansion.'
'And one of the most outspoken voices belonged to Frederick Douglass.'
Would you have me argue that man is entitled to liberty?
'Douglass, a former slave, had fled north to freedom and had become one of our nation's leading advocates for ending slavery.'
To do so would be to make myself ridiculous, and to offer an insult to your understanding.
There is not a man beneath the canopy of heaven who does not know that slavery is wrong for him.
Must I argue the wrongfulness of slavery?
'Douglass, having experienced the brutalities of slavery, was calling for me and all of America to act.'
'I knew it was important to prevent the expansion of slavery, but the cost of it—war—weighed on me.'
'Those in the South were not evil; they had been my fellow Americans just months earlier. I wanted to prevent the war from escalating.'
'But how could I allow **anyone** to attack my country's soil and not take action against the aggressors?'
'I considered **every** possible option.'

Months later.
I suggested to the president that we should get involved in a foreign war. It might be the answer to end our civil war.
You mean find a way to unite the North and South against a common foe?
Yes, but he would not hear of that. He appreciates the concern expressed by England and France, and wants us to remain on good terms with foreign leaders. Maybe we could--
What's that ringing? Is that the bell used to summon White House staffers?
It sounds like more than one bell.
RIIIIINNNNGGG!
It sounds like every bell is ringing!
What could have happened? Is it an emergency?

'But of course when the White House erupted with the ringing of bells that day, sending the staff into a panic, it wasn't an emergency. It was just...'
Your son, Tad, Mr. President. He was playing a practical joke and ringing all the bells after he found the controls in the attic.
He rang the bells for every White House office?
HA HA HA!
'Of course I was never bothered by your little jokes.'
'I wanted you and your brothers to feel at home in the White House and to come and go as you pleased—even if I was in the middle of an important meeting.'
What is it, Willie? What do you want?
I just wanted to give you a hug, Father.
'With soldiers dying across the country... so much loss... I loved having you and your brothers close to me.'

'But soon loss came to our home as well. On February 20, 1862, your brother Willie died from a disease similar to typhoid.'
My poor boy. He was too good for this world!
'I know the two of you were best friends and remember how devastated you were, Tad... how devastated we all were.'
'The loss of a second son absolutely destroyed your mother. She put an end to all social outings. Willie had only been sick a couple weeks, and we weren't prepared to lose him.'
Mary? Mary, talk to me.
'She remained in mourning for an entire year and even visited spiritualists regularly, in the hope that the mediums might give her news of Willie from beyond.'
Is Willie with us? In this room?
He is. And he's well. But he doesn't have a message for you just yet.

Weeks later.
No Robert, I will not allow it!!!
Our country is at war, Mother! I just want to do my part. I want to leave college to serve in the army!
I forbid it, Robert. It's too dangerous. I have buried two of my sons! I will not bury another!
I will not see you come to harm!
'I understood Mary's desire to keep Robert safe and close to home.'
'But while Mary had withdrawn from life and focused all her attentions on you and Robert, I could not allow myself to do the same.'
'I was the president of a nation. I could not forsake my duty. I could not give in to the Confederate States of America.'
'I could not give up my principles and belief that slavery was wrong. I could not allow our country to split permanently. I had to find a way to win the war.'

'I had hoped victory would come through my armies led by General George McClellan.'
'He was then serving a dual role as field commander of my largest army on the east coast, the Army of the Potomac, and as general-in-chief in charge of all Union armies.'
'But victory on the battlefield did not happen.'
'McClellan's strategy was hesitant and cautious.'
Why are General McClellan's forces not advancing?!
He sends word that his troops are exhausted, and their supplies are depleted, Mr. President.
March 1862.
'Week after week we got news of a dithering army. And my frustration over our lack of progress was mounting.'
The general says the horses are fatigued and need to rest, Mr. President.
Perhaps he is not the right man for this job.
I will relieve General McClellan of his role as general-in-chief, but he will still control the Army of the Potomac.
'Yet for all of my frustrations with McClellan's inaction... I knew there were countless others complaining of my own lack of action.'

'In the South, runaway slaves fleeing the plantations would find refuge in the homes of abolitionists and former slaves.'
Hurry! Get inside. I hear the slave masters approaching.
'This network of brave men and women, called the Underground Railroad, provided food, money, and lodging while escorting runaway slaves up north to freedom...'
'...and hiding them from the slave masters and plantation owners.'
WOOF!
WOOF!
'The abolitionists were frustrated with my presidency because slavery still existed. And there were others just as frustrated.
Rochester in New York.
President Lincoln is not doing enough!
Trying to free the slaves a few at a time when there are thousands in need... we need Lincoln to act.
We need him to free all the slaves, and I don't know why he is moving so slowly on this matter.
'What my critics did not realize was that I was reaching the very same conclusion that they were.'

July 1862.
We will free the slaves.
To weaken the Southern Confederacy, we will free the slaves —the backbone of the Southern economy.
'I intended to apply my idea to the Southern states that had seceded. There were still a few Southern slave states along the North-South border that had not rebelled, and I wanted to keep their loyalty and support.'
The South views the slaves not as men, but as property. And we are at war with them. Well, in times of war, property can be seized.
The Southern states that have seceded can lay down their arms and rejoin the Union...
...or every slave in their states will be declared free **permanently**.
'While I spent time working out the details of this new idea, which I called the Emancipation Proclamation, battle after battle were still being fought for the fate of our nation.'

'September 17, 1862 was the bloodiest day of fighting in the state of Maryland.'
'General Lee's Southern forces had hoped to advance north into Maryland, and McClellan, still serving as a field commander, was trying to hold them back.'
'In the Battle of Antietam that ensued, there were massive casualties on both sides, with 23,000 soldiers killed or wounded in just twelve hours of fighting.'
'And when Lee's tired and battered Confederate soldiers made their retreat after failing to advance north...'
'...General McClellan opted against pursuing them because his soldiers were fatigued.'
'It was yet another lost opportunity.'
September 22, 1862.
It's high time we did something. We will give the Confederacy one hundred days to surrender, until January 1. If they don't, we will issue the Emancipation Proclamation and free all the Southern slaves.
Weeks later. November 5, 1862.
Battles are raging still. And McClellan remains ineffective.
I know. I have little choice but to remove McClellan immediately from his command.

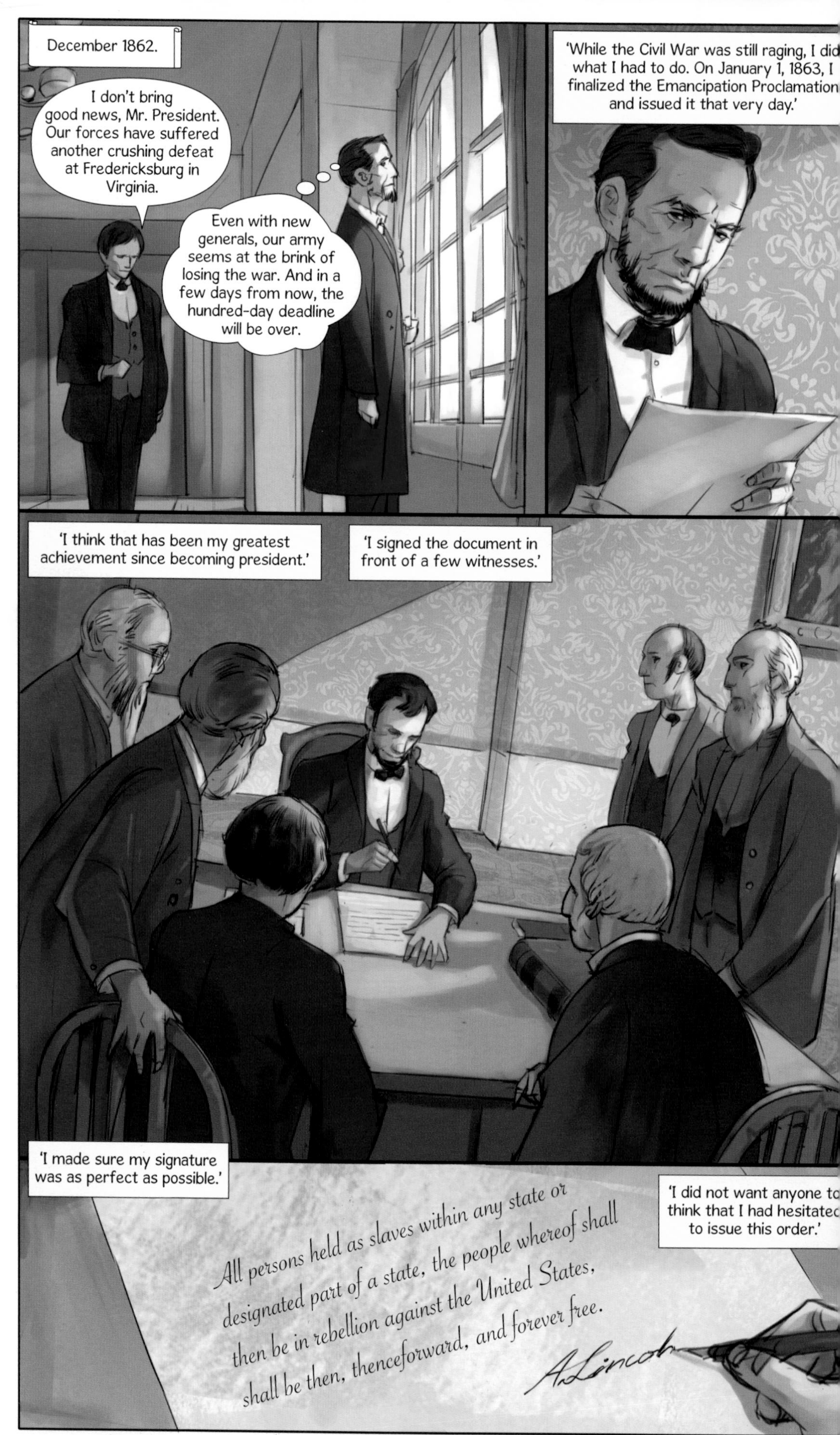
December 1862.
I don't bring good news, Mr. President. Our forces have suffered another crushing defeat at Fredericksburg in Virginia.
Even with new generals, our army seems at the brink of losing the war. And in a few days from now, the hundred-day deadline will be over.
'While the Civil War was still raging, I did what I had to do. On January 1, 1863, I finalized the Emancipation Proclamation and issued it that very day.'
'I think that has been my greatest achievement since becoming president.'
'I signed the document in front of a few witnesses.'
'I made sure my signature was as perfect as possible.'
'I did not want anyone to think that I had hesitated to issue this order.'
All persons held as slaves within any state or designated part of a state, the people whereof shall then be in rebellion against the United States, shall be then, thenceforward, and forever free.
A. Lincoln

Hours later, at an abolition rally in Boston, Massachusetts.
Lincoln is freeing the slaves. Freedom! Finally freedom!
Not complete freedom. Not yet. Lincoln's Proclamation only frees the slaves in the seceding Southern states. But...
What do you think of the news, Mr. Douglass?
I think it is a step in the right direction.
This war is not just for preserving the Union and allowing the South to rejoin the North while keeping its slave system intact.
This war is now also a war **against** slavery, a war **for** freedom. It is a war for what is right and just.
'But unfortunately, the South did not view it that way.'

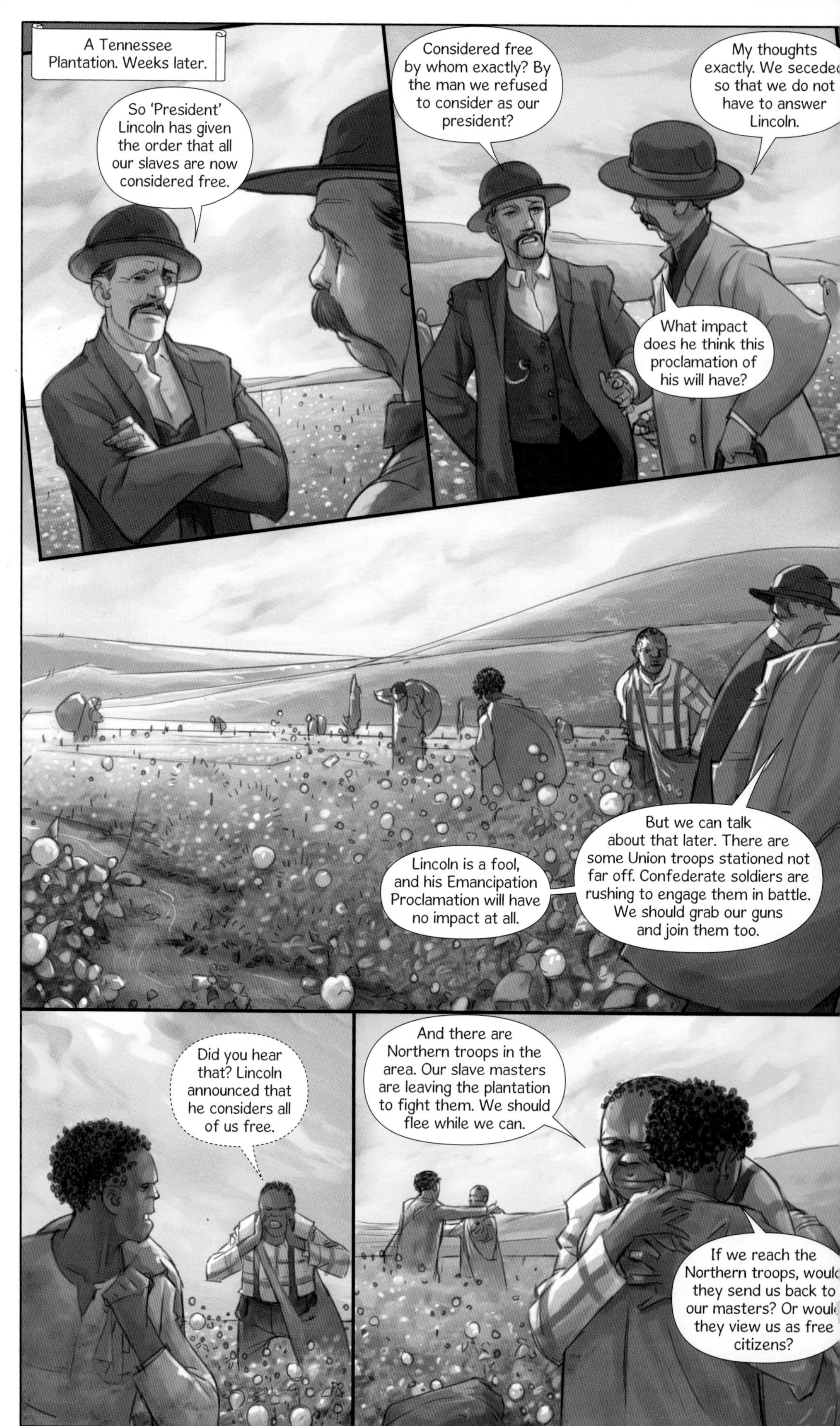

A Tennessee Plantation. Weeks later.
So 'President' Lincoln has given the order that all our slaves are now considered free.
Considered free by whom exactly? By the man we refused to consider as our president?
My thoughts exactly. We secede so that we do not have to answer Lincoln.
What impact does he think this proclamation of his will have?
Lincoln is a fool, and his Emancipation Proclamation will have no impact at all.
But we can talk about that later. There are some Union troops stationed not far off. Confederate soldiers are rushing to engage them in battle. We should grab our guns and join them too.
Did you hear that? Lincoln announced that he considers all of us free.
And there are Northern troops in the area. Our slave masters are leaving the plantation to fight them. We should flee while we can.
If we reach the Northern troops, woul they send us back to our masters? Or woul they view us as free citizens?

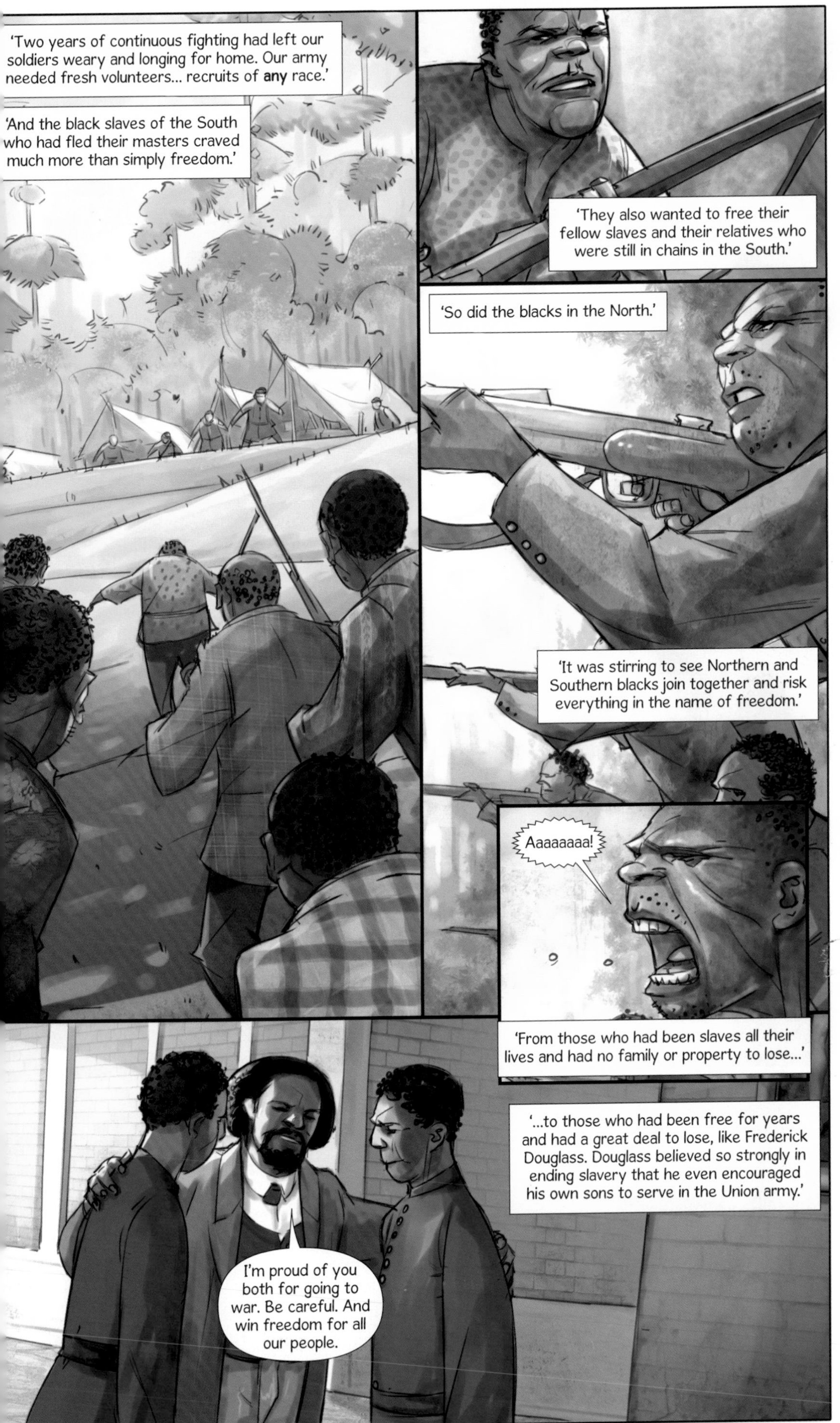
'Two years of continuous fighting had left our soldiers weary and longing for home. Our army needed fresh volunteers... recruits of **any** race.'
'And the black slaves of the South who had fled their masters craved much more than simply freedom.'
'They also wanted to free their fellow slaves and their relatives who were still in chains in the South.'
'So did the blacks in the North.'
'It was stirring to see Northern and Southern blacks join together and risk everything in the name of freedom.'
Aaaaaaaa!
'From those who had been slaves all their lives and had no family or property to lose...'
'...to those who had been free for years and had a great deal to lose, like Frederick Douglass. Douglass believed so strongly in ending slavery that he even encouraged his own sons to serve in the Union army.'
I'm proud of you both for going to war. Be careful. And win freedom for all our people.

'But winning freedom was not an easy thing.'
'The losses mounted. There were more than 200,000 dead since the siege of Fort Sumter.'
'I knew that many of those who were fighting for the chance to be free would probably not experience that freedom.'
'White or black, North or South, it seemed more and more that on the battlefield, there was just death.'
'And every death, every loss weighed heavily on my mind with each order I gave out.'

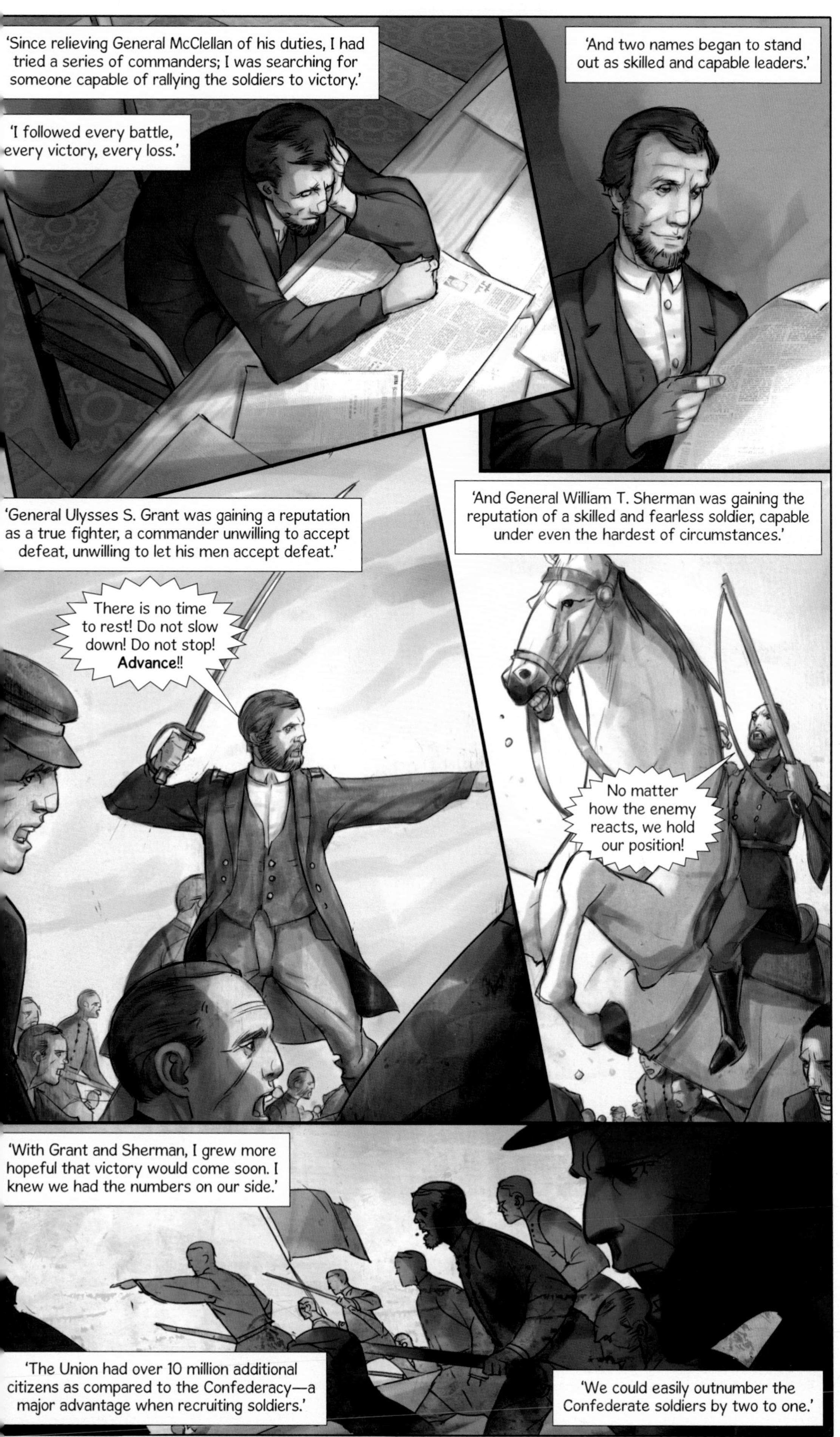
'Since relieving General McClellan of his duties, I had tried a series of commanders; I was searching for someone capable of rallying the soldiers to victory.'
'I followed every battle, every victory, every loss.'
'And two names began to stand out as skilled and capable leaders.'
'General Ulysses S. Grant was gaining a reputation as a true fighter, a commander unwilling to accept defeat, unwilling to let his men accept defeat.'
There is no time to rest! Do not slow down! Do not stop! **Advance**!!
'And General William T. Sherman was gaining the reputation of a skilled and fearless soldier, capable under even the hardest of circumstances.'
No matter how the enemy reacts, we hold our position!
'With Grant and Sherman, I grew more hopeful that victory would come soon. I knew we had the numbers on our side.'
'The Union had over 10 million additional citizens as compared to the Confederacy—a major advantage when recruiting soldiers.'
'We could easily outnumber the Confederate soldiers by two to one.'

'But despite being outnumbered and outgunned, the South did not back down.'
'And with General Robert E. Lee leading them, they began pushing north as they had done at Antietam, again harboring plans to invade our Northern states.'
Fire!!
'The two armies met at Gettysburg in Pennsylvania on July 1, 1863, and fought for three days. It was a town of 2,500 invaded suddenly by 165,000 soldiers.'
'The war between the North and South that had divided our nation had also divided families and friends, who were now separated by the North-South boundary.'
'Whether on the field at Gettysburg or at one of the countless other battles, there was virtually no one in the country who did not have loved ones fighting in the war, sometimes on both sides. It was a sorry sight—literally brother killing brother.'
'The family of Anne Rutledge was fighting for the North. Mary Owens, who had moved to the South, had her sons fighting for the Confederacy.'
*The Confederate flag shown on this page was so designed by the secessionists to avoid confusion with the Union flag for they looked similar.

'Your mother's family was a slave-owning family. Her family, too, opposed my anti-slavery policies and fought against my armies.'
'Her half-brothers died fighting for the Confederacy. Many Southerners viewed your mother as a traitor for siding with the North during the war. Everyone chose a side. And there could only be one victor. It was the deciding point.'
'At Gettysburg... we emerged the victors. Of course, victors might not be an accurate choice of word when there were more than 50,000 casualties. But we finally forced General Lee to abandon his plans to invade the North.'

'Months later, I returned to Gettysburg to deliver my speech in memory of the soldiers who had fought for the noble cause.'
November 19, 1863. Gettysburg in Pennsylvania.
Four score and seven years ago our fathers brought forth upon this continent a new nation, conceived in liberty, and dedicated to the proposition that all men are created equal.
Now we are engaged in a great civil war, testing whether that nation, or any nation so conceived and so dedicated, can long endure. We are met on a great battlefield of that war.
We have come to dedicate a portion of that field as a final resting place for those who here gave their lives that the nation might live. The world will little note, nor long remember what we say here, but it can never forget what they did here.
We here highly resolve these dead shall not have died in vain, that this nation, under God, shall have a new birth of freedom, and that government of the people, by the people, for the people shall not perish from the earth.
'Gettysburg had been just one battle. The hope was that if we held true to the belief that slavery was wrong, we could eventually prevail over the South, win the war, end slavery, and reunite the nation.'

March 1864.
You seem troubled, Abe.
The war is costing us 2 million dollars a day. I will be up for re-election this year, and my popularity is dropping.
I am troubled, Mary. I have been president for three years now. And I hear only criticism about me.
For three years our nation has been at war, with no end in sight. Politicians and reporters say I am not doing all I should to end the war. They think I should give in on the slavery issue.
Do you have any idea who might be running against you in the next election?
There are rumors swirling around Washington that both the Republican and Democratic parties want Ulysses S. Grant, my own general, to run against me. His courage in battle has gained him the respect of the soldiers.
He is skilled at commanding the soldiers, and I need him as a general. But is he loyal? Or will he stand against me?
I need to know his thoughts on this.

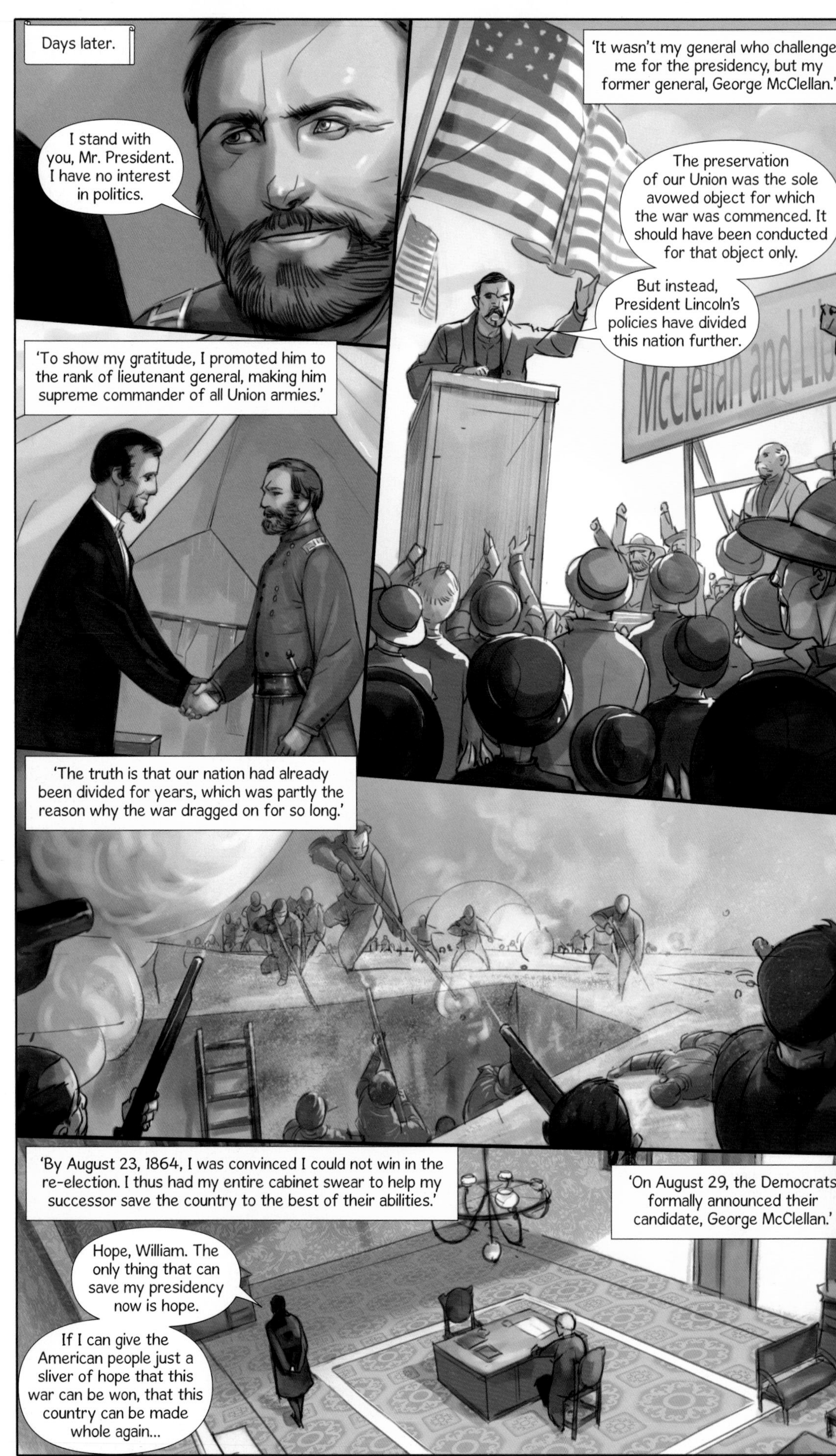
Days later.
I stand with you, Mr. President. I have no interest in politics.
'It wasn't my general who challenged me for the presidency, but my former general, George McClellan.'
The preservation of our Union was the sole avowed object for which the war was commenced. It should have been conducted for that object only.
But instead, President Lincoln's policies have divided this nation further.
McClellan and Lib
'To show my gratitude, I promoted him to the rank of lieutenant general, making him supreme commander of all Union armies.'
'The truth is that our nation had already been divided for years, which was partly the reason why the war dragged on for so long.'
'By August 23, 1864, I was convinced I could not win in the re-election. I thus had my entire cabinet swear to help my successor save the country to the best of their abilities.'
'On August 29, the Democrats formally announced their candidate, George McClellan.'
Hope, William. The only thing that can save my presidency now is hope.
If I can give the American people just a sliver of hope that this war can be won, that this country can be made whole again...

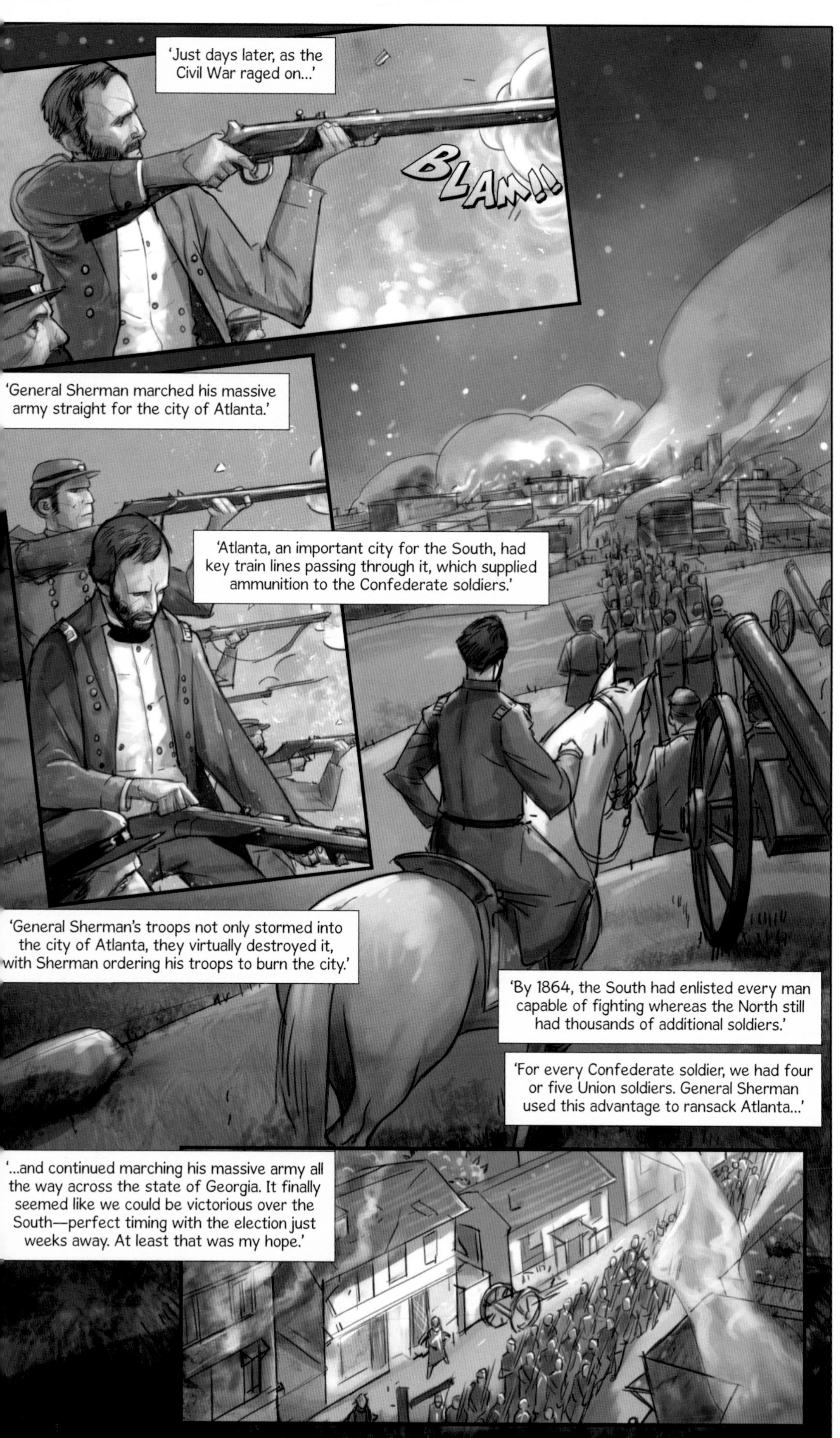
'Just days later, as the Civil War raged on...'
BLAM!!
'General Sherman marched his massive army straight for the city of Atlanta.'
'Atlanta, an important city for the South, had key train lines passing through it, which supplied ammunition to the Confederate soldiers.'
'General Sherman's troops not only stormed into the city of Atlanta, they virtually destroyed it, with Sherman ordering his troops to burn the city.'
'By 1864, the South had enlisted every man capable of fighting whereas the North still had thousands of additional soldiers.'
'For every Confederate soldier, we had four or five Union soldiers. General Sherman used this advantage to ransack Atlanta...'
'...and continued marching his massive army all the way across the state of Georgia. It finally seemed like we could be victorious over the South—perfect timing with the election just weeks away. At least that was my hope.'

'My brief time serving in the Black Hawk War had taught me how hard a war can be on a soldier.'
'But as leader of a nation, it was my job to focus on what was best for the entire country, even if it meant that there would be more casualties.'
'The courage of many faltered in the face of personal bereavement.'
This war has claimed my son, and my husband is still fighting on the battlefield. I don't care how the war ends... I just want my husband safe and back.
'And yet many of the soldiers wanted desperately to win the war—an assurance that their comrades had not died in vain.'
'The victory at Atlanta gave our entire nation the hope that we could achieve what was best for the nation as well as for the families of soldiers. And the only time our soldiers left their posts was to cast their votes in the presidential election.'
'Almost 80 percent of the soldiers voted for me, as did a majority of the Union.'
'And so on November 8, 1864, I was elected to serve a second term as president.'
'But it was not an occasion to celebrate, for the Civil War was still going on.'

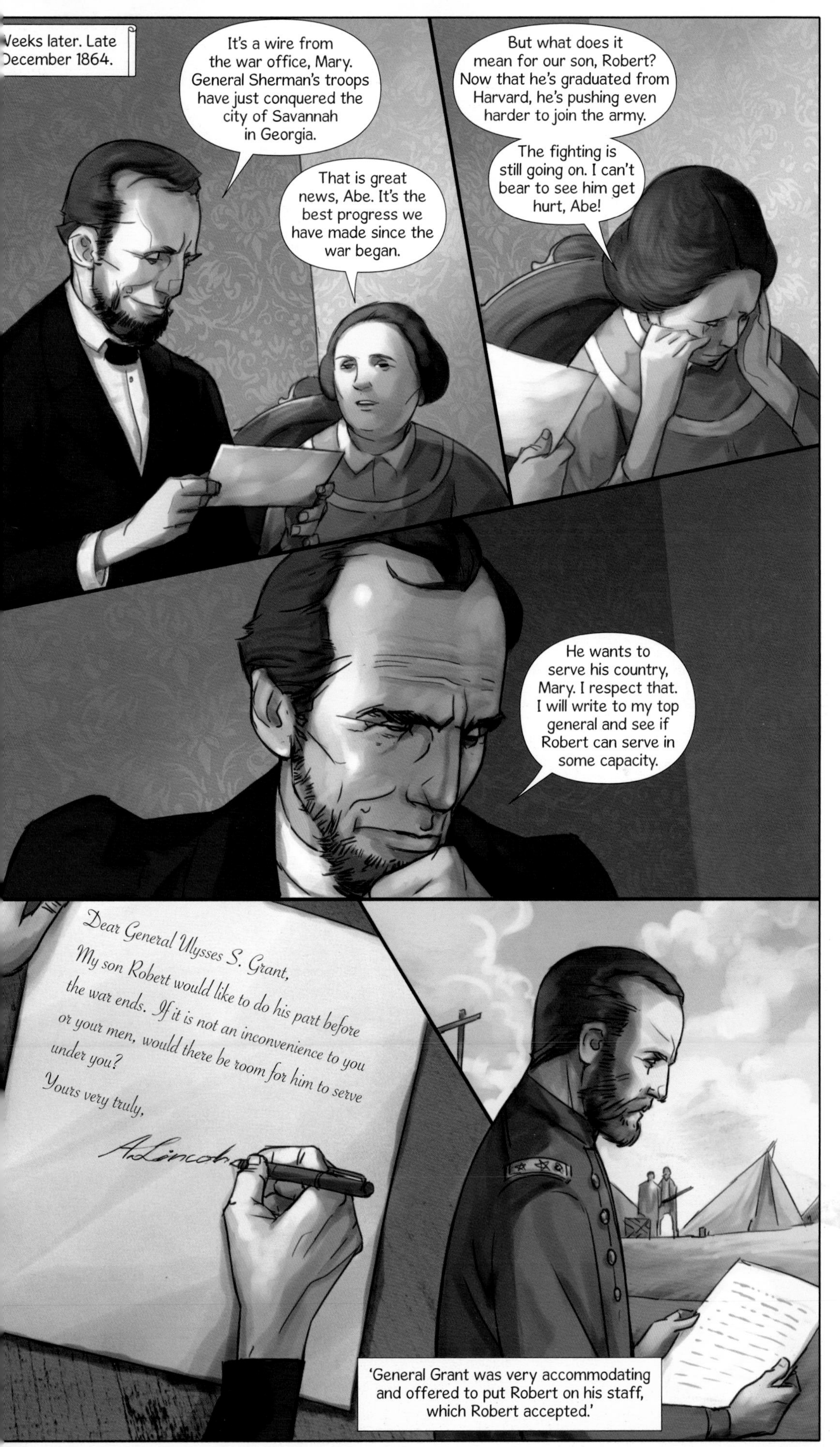
Weeks later. Late December 1864.
It's a wire from the war office, Mary. General Sherman's troops have just conquered the city of Savannah in Georgia.
That is great news, Abe. It's the best progress we have made since the war began.
But what does it mean for our son, Robert? Now that he's graduated from Harvard, he's pushing even harder to join the army.
The fighting is still going on. I can't bear to see him get hurt, Abe!
He wants to serve his country, Mary. I respect that. I will write to my top general and see if Robert can serve in some capacity.
Dear General Ulysses S. Grant,
My son Robert would like to do his part before the war ends. If it is not an inconvenience to you or your men, would there be room for him to serve under you?
Yours very truly,
A. Lincoln
'General Grant was very accommodating and offered to put Robert on his staff, which Robert accepted.'

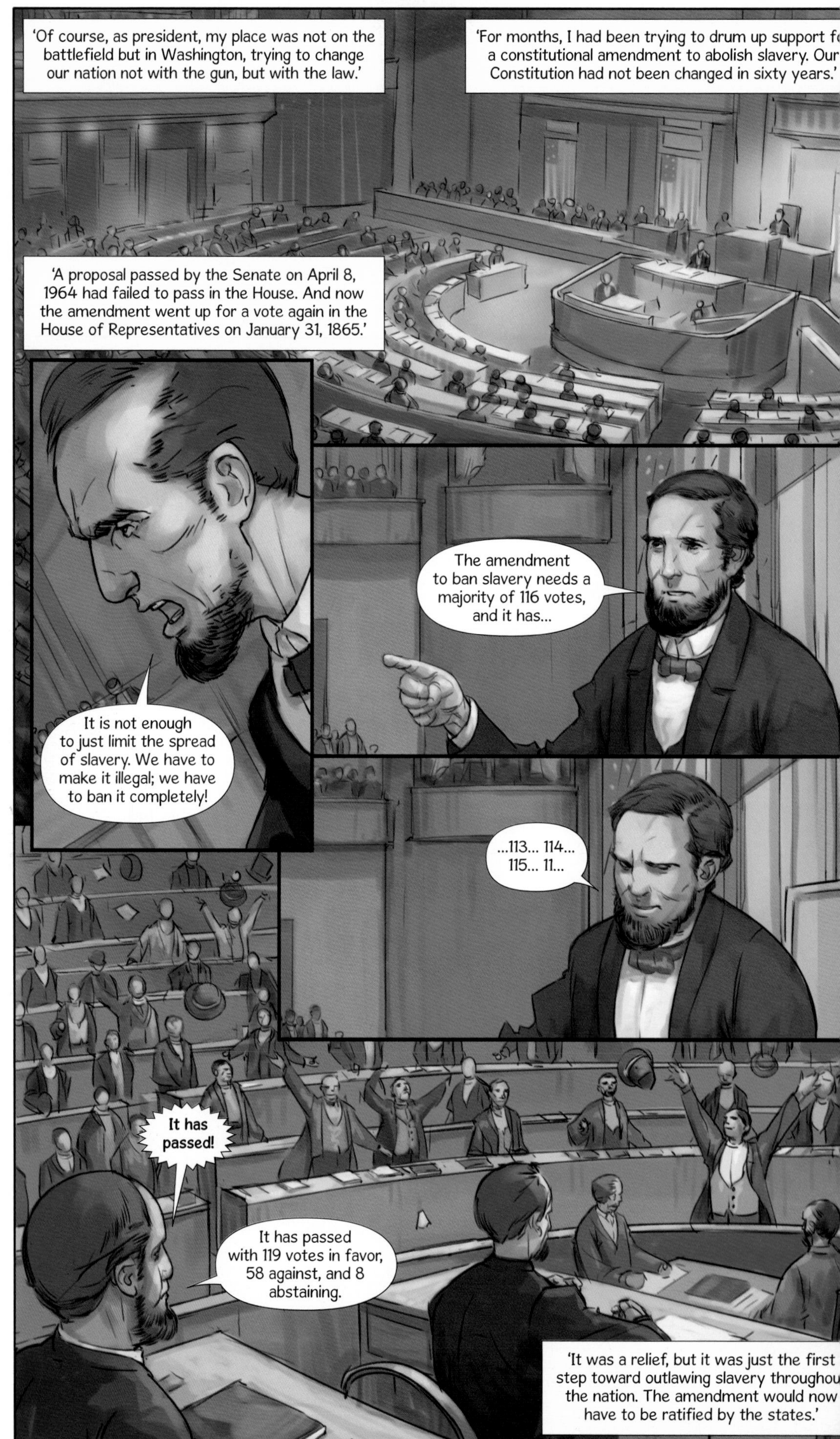
'Of course, as president, my place was not on the battlefield but in Washington, trying to change our nation not with the gun, but with the law.'
'For months, I had been trying to drum up support f a constitutional amendment to abolish slavery. Our Constitution had not been changed in sixty years.'
'A proposal passed by the Senate on April 8, 1964 had failed to pass in the House. And now the amendment went up for a vote again in the House of Representatives on January 31, 1865.'
It is not enough to just limit the spread of slavery. We have to make it illegal; we have to ban it completely!
The amendment to ban slavery needs a majority of 116 votes, and it has...
...113... 114... 115... 11...
It has passed!
It has passed with 119 votes in favor, 58 against, and 8 abstaining.
'It was a relief, but it was just the first step toward outlawing slavery throughou the nation. The amendment would now have to be ratified by the states.'

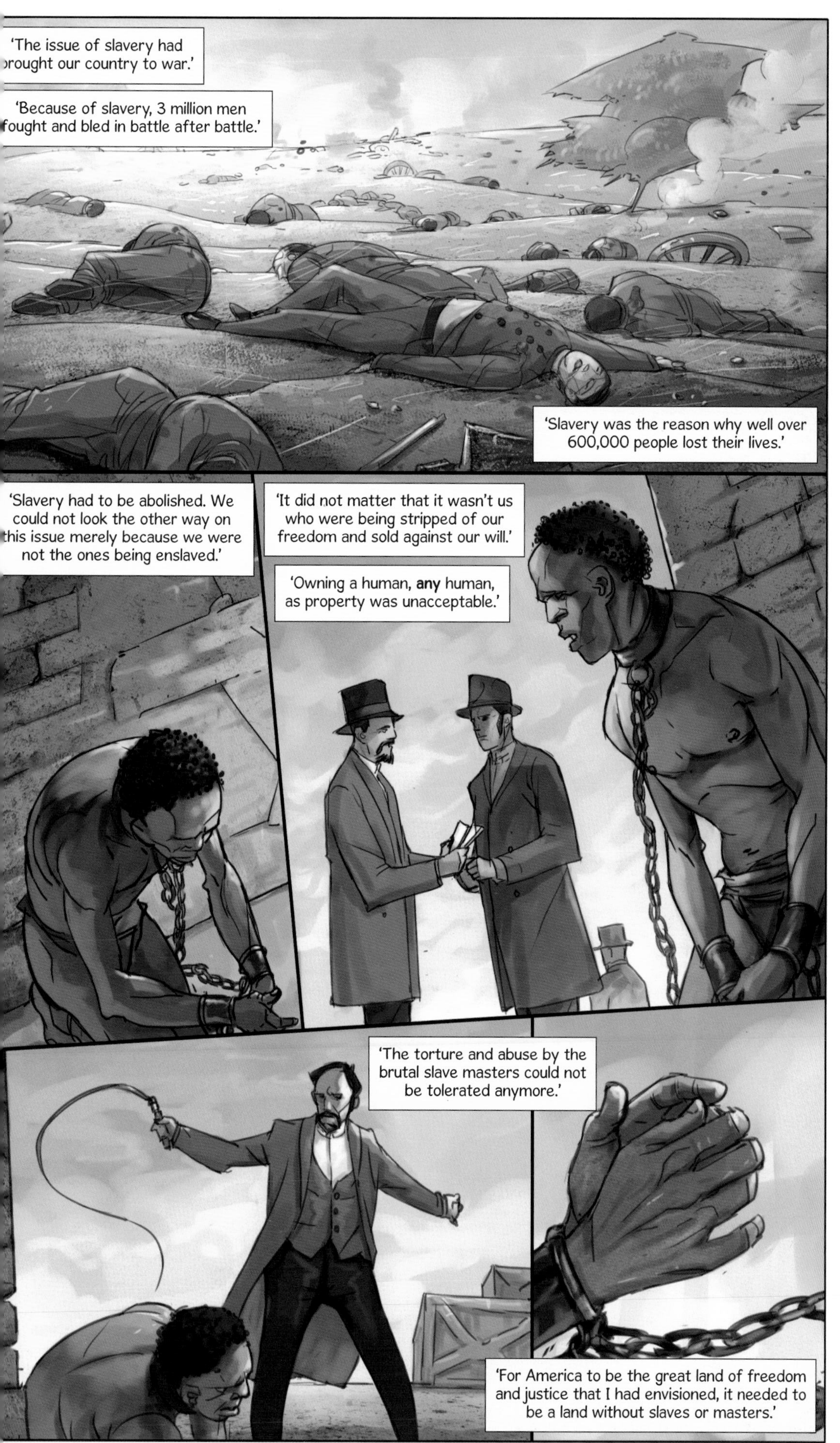
'The issue of slavery had
brought our country to war.'
'Because of slavery, 3 million men
fought and bled in battle after battle.'
'Slavery was the reason why well over
600,000 people lost their lives.'
'Slavery had to be abolished. We
could not look the other way on
this issue merely because we were
not the ones being enslaved.'
'It did not matter that it wasn't us
who were being stripped of our
freedom and sold against our will.'
'Owning a human, **any** human,
as property was unacceptable.'
'The torture and abuse by the
brutal slave masters could not
be tolerated anymore.'
'For America to be the great land of freedom
and justice that I had envisioned, it needed to
be a land without slaves or masters.'

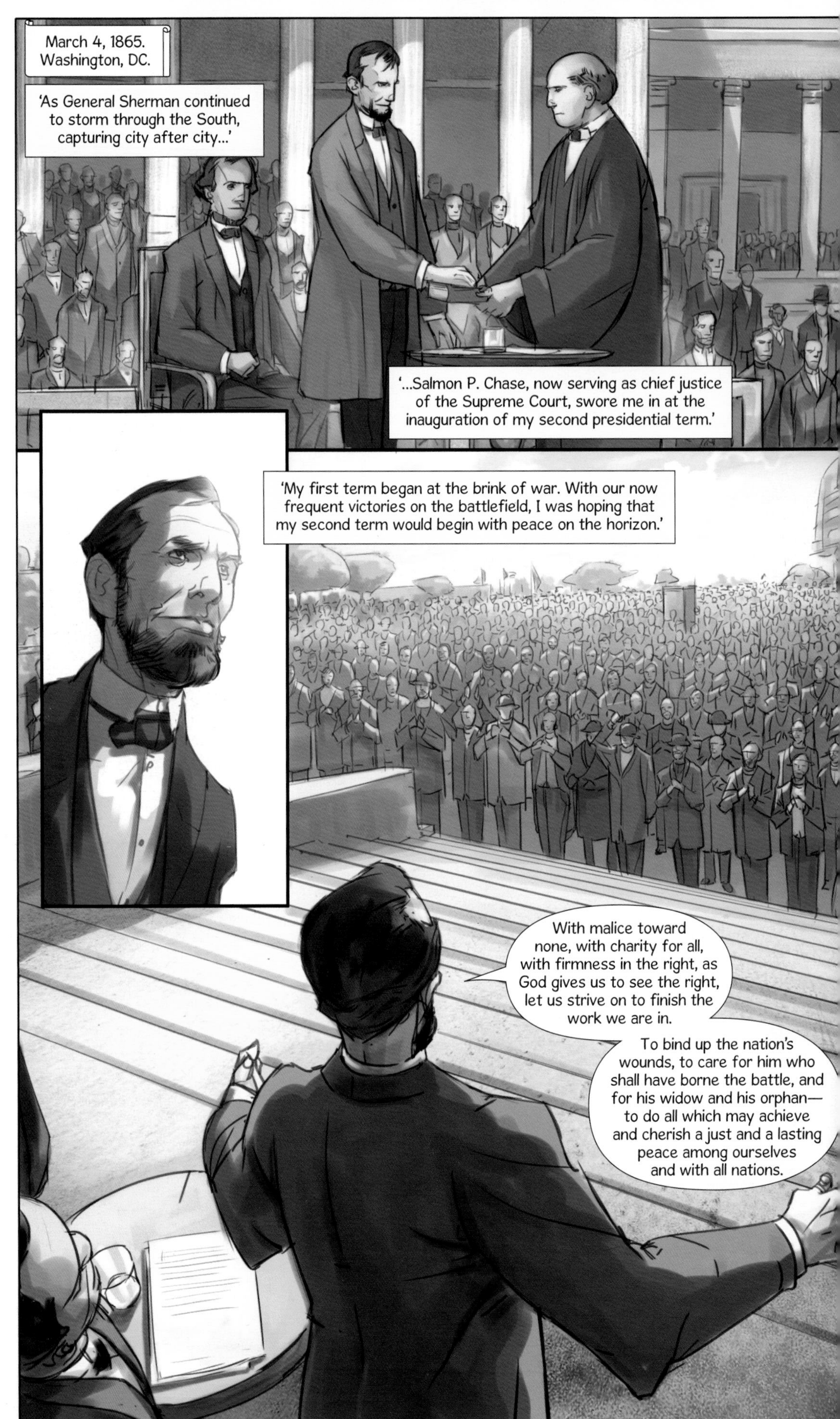
March 4, 1865.
Washington, DC.
'As General Sherman continued to storm through the South, capturing city after city...'
'...Salmon P. Chase, now serving as chief justice of the Supreme Court, swore me in at the inauguration of my second presidential term.'
'My first term began at the brink of war. With our now frequent victories on the battlefield, I was hoping that my second term would begin with peace on the horizon.'
With malice toward none, with charity for all, with firmness in the right, as God gives us to see the right, let us strive on to finish the work we are in.
To bind up the nation's wounds, to care for him who shall have borne the battle, and for his widow and his orphan— to do all which may achieve and cherish a just and a lasting peace among ourselves and with all nations.

Hours later, at a White House reception.
Mr. President, there is a black man at the door being detained by the police. He claims he is Frederick Douglass and was invited here by you.
'I had indeed invited Douglass, a man I had grown to know and respect for his tireless efforts to put an end to slavery.'
Unhand Mr. Douglass at once!
Here comes my friend, Frederick Douglass.
I saw you in the crowd at my inauguration. Tell me, what did you think of my speech?
It was a sacred effort.
I am glad you liked it.
'I had hoped my speech would resonate with those in the crowd, so I appreciated Mr. Douglass's compliment. But he knew as well as I did that we needed more than words and speeches.'
'We still had to end the war. I decided to meet with my top generals personally to determine the next step.'

March 27, 1865. Center Point, Virginia.
General Lee's forces will not escape us, Mr. President. His soldiers are holding their ground here in Virginia, but I'm preparing an assault against them even as we speak.
General Grant is correct, sir. And further south, my units are crushing what resistance they find, and making their way back north. We are confident this war is almost over.
We must be just as confident about how we move forward when the war does end.
How do we unite this country after years of bloodshed? I think when this war is over...
...we must not seek retribution against those who opposed us. There must be no hangings. We have already spilled too much blood.
Lee being Lee, more blood will be shed.
Do you still fear the Confederate soldiers will try and hold their ground, General Grant?

April 4, 1865.
Richmond, Virginia.
'The Southern soldiers did not try to hold their ground. Just a week later, Richmond, the capital city of the Confederacy, fell to our forces.'
'It was not only the Confederate soldiers who fled, but also the Confederate president, Jefferson Davis. And I traveled to Richmond to see our victory firsthand.'
Freedom! Finally, we have freedom!
The South has fallen! Thanks to President Abraham Lincoln fighting against slavery, we are now free.
Look! Bless the Lord, Father Abraham's come.
Thank you for--
You do not need to thank me. You need to only thank God for your freedom.

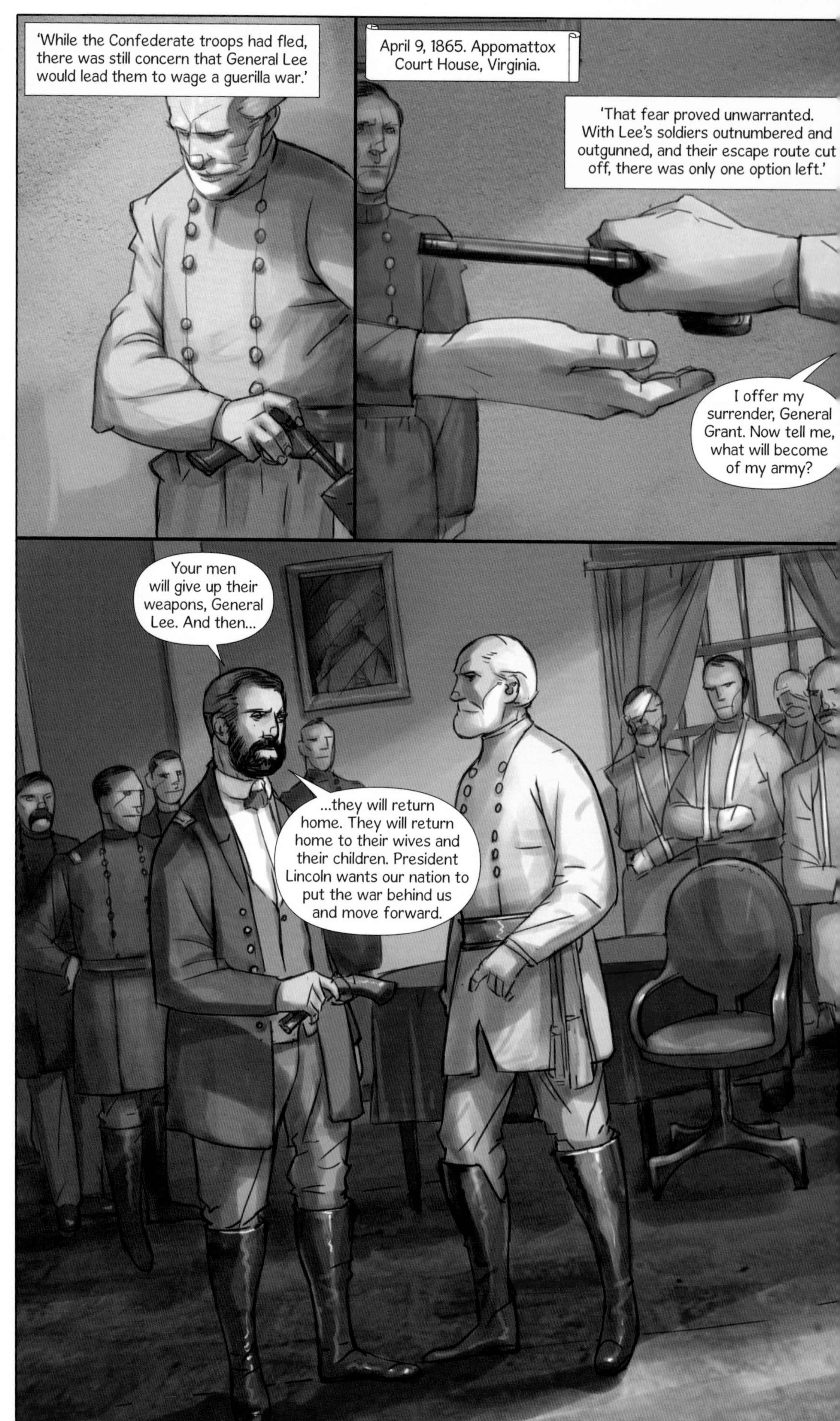
'While the Confederate troops had fled, there was still concern that General Lee would lead them to wage a guerilla war.'
April 9, 1865. Appomattox Court House, Virginia.
'That fear proved unwarranted. With Lee's soldiers outnumbered and outgunned, and their escape route cut off, there was only one option left.'
I offer my surrender, General Grant. Now tell me, what will become of my army?
Your men will give up their weapons, General Lee. And then...
...they will return home. They will return home to their wives and their children. President Lincoln wants our nation to put the war behind us and move forward.

'Though there were still a few groups of rebel soldiers scattered throughout the South and a few small skirmishes, with Lee's surrender...'
'...the war was finally over.'
The war is over!!!
General Lee has surrendered. The war is over!
'So many black men and women had never experienced anything in America but slavery. Enslaved on plantations, many since birth, they had no home of their own, no jobs to go to; their families had been torn apart.'
'After four years of war, and nearly a century of slavery since America had been founded, the nation could not be healed in a single day.'
'But it was a beginning.'
Freedom!

April 14, 1865. The White House, Washington, DC.
But I believe I have spoken long enough, Tad. We need to get ready for the theater, or the play will be over before we get there.
What play are you going to see, Tad?
Your brother is going to see *Aladdin*. And your mother and I are seeing a play called Our *American Cousin*.
Come with me, Robert.
You said earlier you didn't want to join us, Robert. But I'd still love it if you came.
Thank you, Father. But I'm feeling tired tonight. Maybe next time.
If you change your mind, your mother and I will be at Ford's Theatre, just six blocks away. We'll be home soon.
And then tomorrow we can talk about a new time in our country—a time of peace.

But unknown to Lincoln, there was trouble brewing.
There can never be peace! There can never be an end to the war!
Yes, at least not while Lincoln is president. We can never accept him as our president or accept his anti-slavery policies.
There were many determined to do **anything** to ensure that slavery did not end, and that Lincoln did not triumph. John Wilkes Booth and his friend, Lewis Powell, were among them.
As were George Atzerodt and David Herold.
It is agreed then. We will kill President Abraham Lincoln. We will take down the entire government.
The South will rise again, John.
George is right. We will all see to that.

Booth and his allies put their plan in motion on April 14, 1865.
Two of the conspirators, Lewis Powell and David Herold, made their way to the home of Lincoln's closest advisor, Secretary of State William Seward.
Posing as a messenger, Powell gained entry into Seward's home.
I don't see why you can't just give the medicine you're delivering for my father to me.
Your father's doctor said I was to deliver it only to him.
After subduing Seward's son, Frederick...
Aaaiieee!
...Powell entered Seward's bedroom to assassinate him.

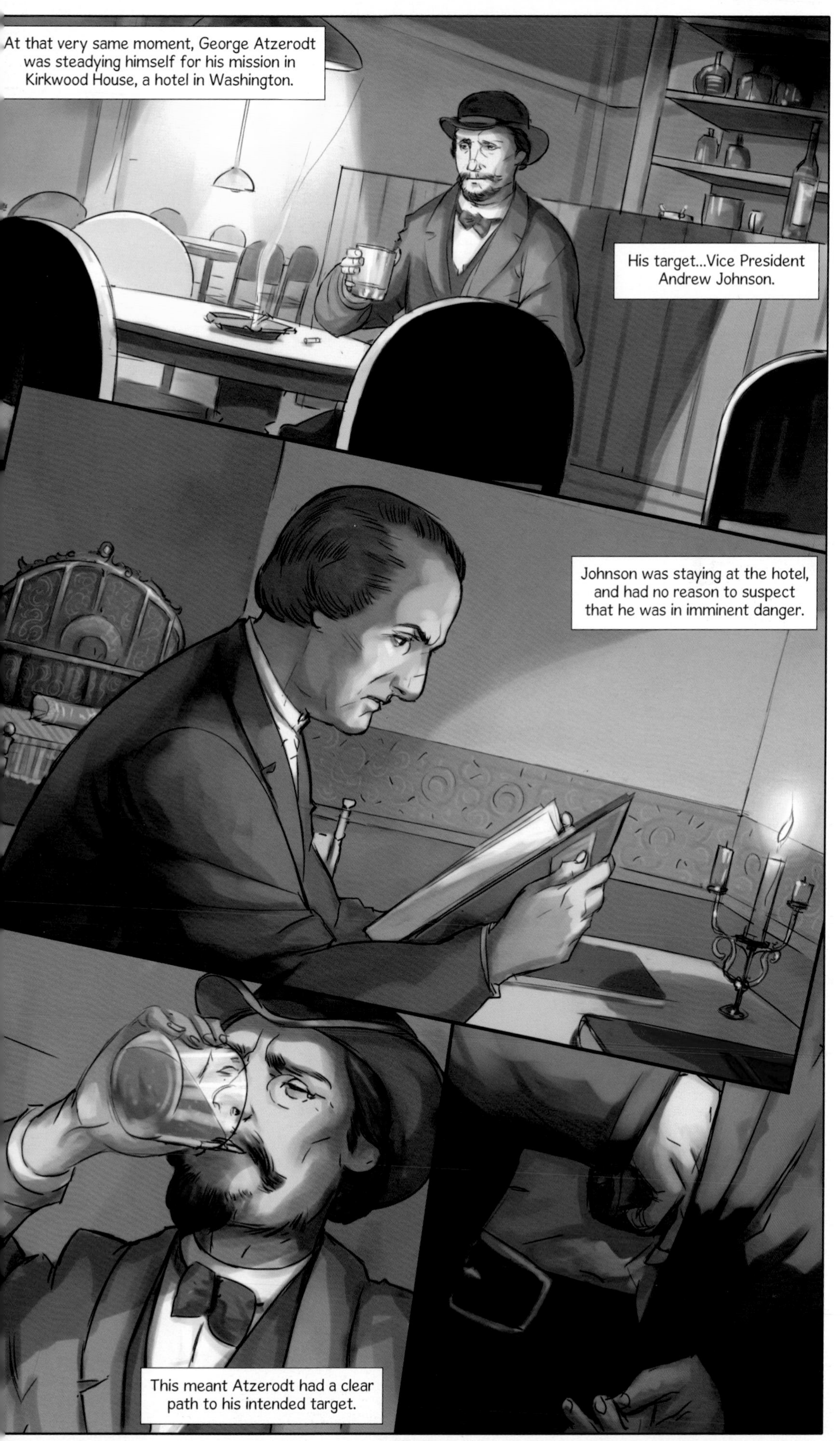
At that very same moment, George Atzerodt was steadying himself for his mission in Kirkwood House, a hotel in Washington.
His target...Vice President Andrew Johnson.
Johnson was staying at the hotel, and had no reason to suspect that he was in imminent danger.
This meant Atzerodt had a clear path to his intended target.

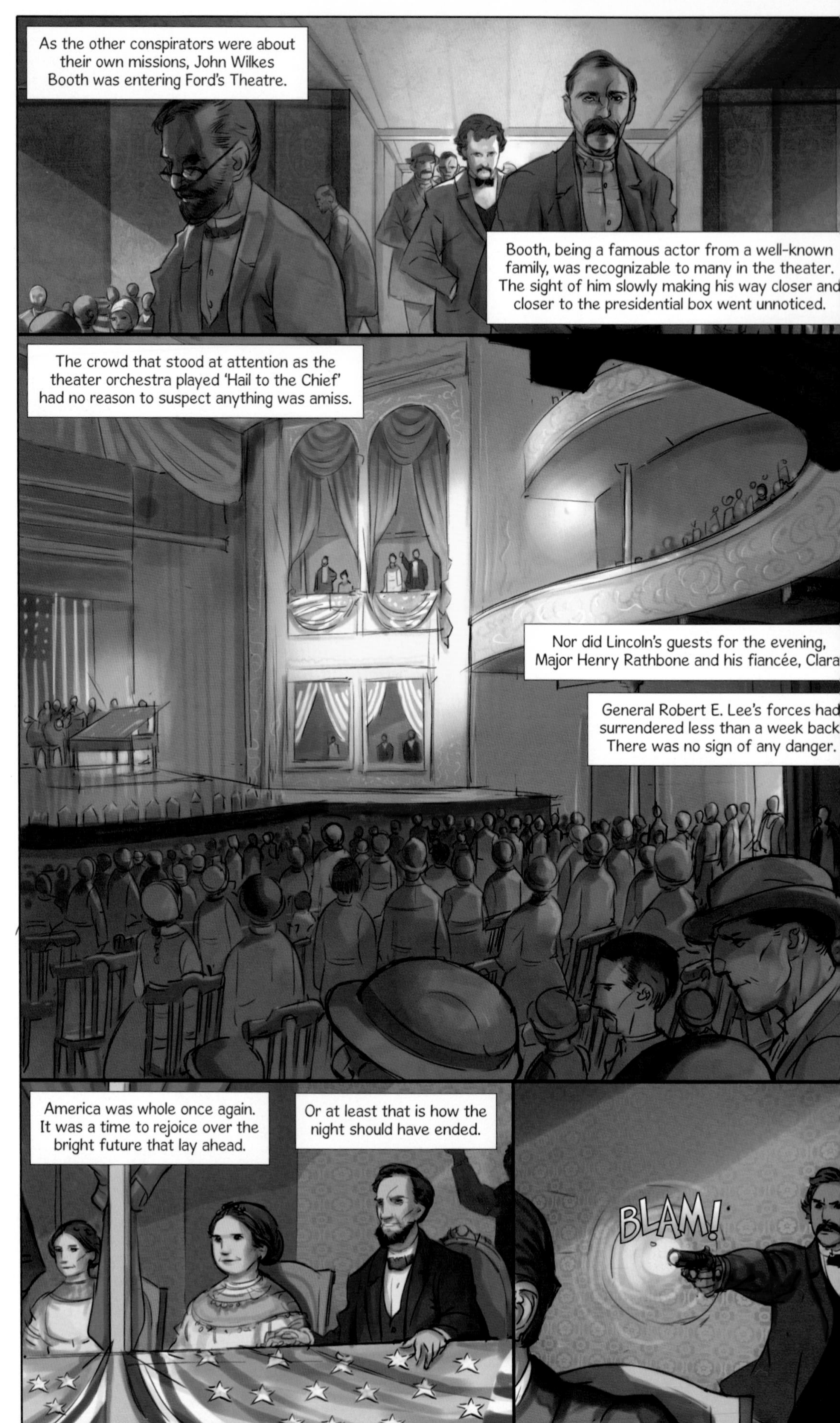
As the other conspirators were about their own missions, John Wilkes Booth was entering Ford's Theatre.
Booth, being a famous actor from a well-known family, was recognizable to many in the theater. The sight of him slowly making his way closer and closer to the presidential box went unnoticed.
The crowd that stood at attention as the theater orchestra played 'Hail to the Chief' had no reason to suspect anything was amiss.
Nor did Lincoln's guests for the evening, Major Henry Rathbone and his fiancée, Clara
General Robert E. Lee's forces had surrendered less than a week back
There was no sign of any danger.
America was whole once again. It was a time to rejoice over the bright future that lay ahead.
Or at least that is how the night should have ended.
BLAM!

Aaaiiieeee!!
The sound of the gunshot and Mary's bloodcurdling scream echoed through the theater.
Booth slashed Major Rathbone's arm with a knife before he dived to make his getaway.
Sic semper tyrannis!*
An awkward landing on the stage from the presidential box left Booth with a broken ankle.
But he limped his way to the back alley where he had left his horse, and rode off into the night.
*Thus always to tyrants!

Back inside the theater, every doctor in attendance rushed to Lincoln's side.
He's not breathing! There's no pulse!!
It looks like the bullet went into the back of his head and is lodged behind his right eye. There's a blood clot on the wound.
If we can remove the clot, it might ease some pressure on his brain. Then if we can get him breathing again...
But the desperate attempt to revive the fallen leader brought little hope for recovery.
There's a faint breath but... he's still in bad shape. We need more room to work. We have to get him out of here.

The president was carried to a boarding house across the street from the theater, and as surgeons and doctors hurried to his side, word of the assassination attempt began to spread throughout the city.
Everyone out of the way! Clear a path!
Young Tad was rushed back to the safety of the White House by the tutor who had accompanied him to the theater...
...while Robert Todd Lincoln rushed to his father's bedside.
No! Oh, no!

The wound appears fatal.
I'm not sure if there's much we can do for him.
It was not only Lincoln's eldest son who had rushed over upon hearing the news.
Politicians and cabinet members from all over Washington made their way to Lincoln's side, including Edwin Stanton, the secretary of war.
There is more news, Mr. Stanton.
It was not just President Lincoln who was attacked. William Seward was stabbed in his home five times.
Amazingly, he survived the attack. The details are still coming in.
I want every road out of Washington sealed off. That is an order
No one gets out of this city! **No one!!**

But the conspirators
were already on the run.
David Herold, stationed outside Seward's house during the attack, hadn't even waited for his accomplice to come out. He fled the moment he heard the ear-piercing screams.
Powell, too, fled from Seward's house, thinking the secretary of state to be dead.
Fortunately, he had only disfigured Seward's face.
George Atzerodt, who had been assigned to kill Vice President Andrew Johnson, backed out of the mission at the last moment and spent his night drinking.
Only John Wilkes Booth succeeded in his mission for at 7:22 a.m. on April 15, 1865...
...Abraham Lincoln became the first American president to be assassinated.

For more than four years, the entire country had remained in a continuous state of mourning as one battle after another claimed the lives of countless fathers and brothers, uncles and sons.
The war was over now, yet the country remained in mourning. They were mourning for one who had guided them through the darkest of times that America had ever seen.
Led by a unit of black soldiers who were the first to take control of the Confederate capitol of Richmond weeks earlier, the funeral procession drew tens of thousands who lined the streets of Washington to have a last glimpse of their beloved president.
The nation grieved... but they also yearned for justice for President Lincoln as his killers were still on the loose.

The conspirators, who had been on the run since April 14, were identified and hunted down, one by one.
Get on the ground, or I'll fire!
On April 26, 1865, David Herold and John Wilkes Booth were found hiding on a farm in Port Royal in Virginia.
David Herold surrendered.
Booth had shaved off his mustache to avoid identification. Though surrounded by soldiers, he had no intention of surrendering.
The shed he was hiding in was put on fire in an attempt to draw him out. However, he was shot dead while still inside the shed.
A total of ten conspirators were uncovered, and those playing a minor role were sentenced to life in prison.
The ones who took a lead in the assassination plot—like Herold, Powell, and Atzerodt—were sentenced to die and were executed.

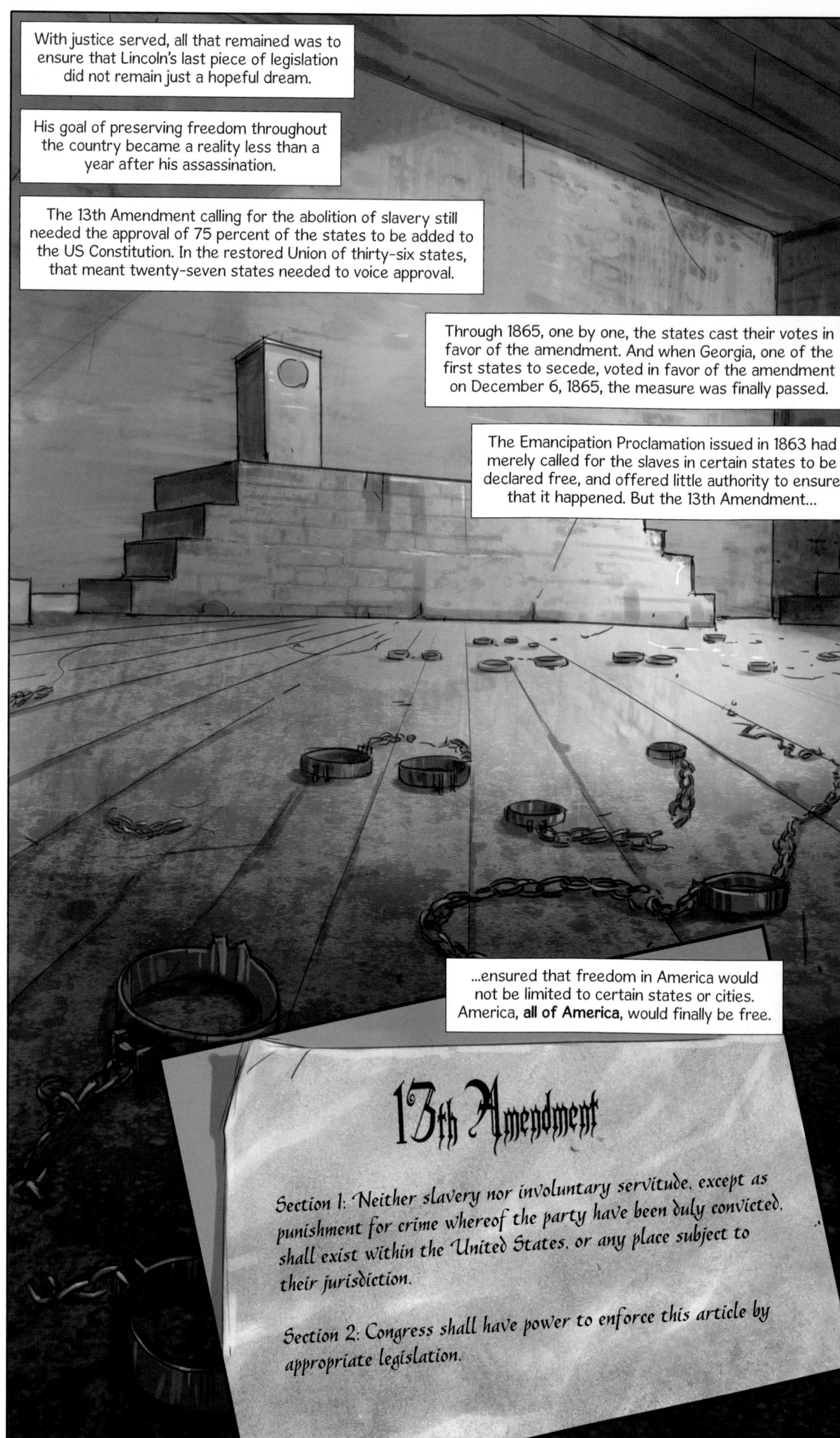
With justice served, all that remained was to ensure that Lincoln's last piece of legislation did not remain just a hopeful dream.
His goal of preserving freedom throughout the country became a reality less than a year after his assassination.
The 13th Amendment calling for the abolition of slavery still needed the approval of 75 percent of the states to be added to the US Constitution. In the restored Union of thirty-six states, that meant twenty-seven states needed to voice approval.
Through 1865, one by one, the states cast their votes in favor of the amendment. And when Georgia, one of the first states to secede, voted in favor of the amendment on December 6, 1865, the measure was finally passed.
The Emancipation Proclamation issued in 1863 had merely called for the slaves in certain states to be declared free, and offered little authority to ensure that it happened. But the 13th Amendment...
...ensured that freedom in America would not be limited to certain states or cities. America, **all of America,** would finally be free.
13th Amendment
Section 1: Neither slavery nor involuntary servitude, except as punishment for crime whereof the party have been duly convicted, shall exist within the United States, or any place subject to their jurisdiction.
Section 2: Congress shall have power to enforce this article by appropriate legislation.

With her husband gone and his work now finished, Mary left Washington, never to return.
Her young son, Tad, passed away just six years after Lincoln's assassination, making him the third of her four sons not to reach the age of twenty.
Mary died in 1882 at her sister's home in Springfield—the very place where she first met 'Honest Abe'.
Robert followed in the footsteps of his father. He became a lawyer and did return to Washington, serving four years as the US secretary of war.
And he was in attendance in 1922 for the dedication of the Lincoln Memorial, a monument built to help preserve the legacy of President Abraham Lincoln.
A legacy that continues to this very day...

Well over a century later, US President Bill Clinton kept a draft of the Gettysburg Address on his desk.
It served as a reminder of Lincoln's spirit and determination, a reminder of the greatness that leaders are capable of.
When preparing to take office as the 44th US president, Barack Obama, too, looked to Lincoln for inspiration.
Abraham Lincoln
When deciding whom he would ask to serve in his cabinet and help lead the nation, he chose to select the best, even if that meant his fiercest rivals.
He filled his cabinet with members of both political parties. He appointed Senator Hillary Clinton, his main opponent and critic within his own party, as his secretary of state.
So why do modern-day leaders still look to Abraham Lincoln's actions for guidance?

Perhaps that is because Abraham Lincoln's actions show us that we should always strive to be guided by the better angels of our nature.
A self-educated and self-made man, Lincoln could not accept that his future lay on the farms or on the frontiers.
Nor could he accept that the future of his nation should be resigned to slavery and injustice.
Abraham Lincoln showed us that even in the darkest of times, when our minds are filled with doubt and nearly **everything** in life seems uncertain...
...if we hold true to our convictions and remain willing to fight for our beliefs, we can never lose our way.

A Man of Many Colors

You know about Abraham Lincoln, the man who brought an end to slavery, the determined politician, and the loving father and husband. But did you know the following things about him?

Lincoln the Inventor

Abraham Lincoln was also a proficient inventor. He was fond of technology, and on May 22, 1849, he managed to get a patent, the first American president to do so, for a device that could lift steamboats over shoals. Unfortunately, the device was never manufactured, and the world never knew that Lincoln was a master inventor!

Lincoln's Multipurpose Hat

Lincoln wearing his stovepipe hat, named so on account of its unusual height, is one of the most iconic historical images. However, it seems it wasn't just a hat, but an extra pocket! It was used for carrying letters, notes, bills, and even important legal documents!

Lincoln and the Supernatural

Abe Lincoln had a close relationship with the supernatural. A firm believer in premonitions, he foresaw his death in dreams twice—the first a week before the assassination, and the second on the fateful day itself!

Lincoln also dabbled in the occult with his wife. The Lincolns were close associates of Paschal Beverly Randolph, who founded the oldest American Rosicrucian Order, and they performed seances at the White House.